Multicultural Literature Collection

MEXICAN AMERICAN LITERATURE

GLOBE BOOK COMPANY

Executive Editor: Virginia Seeley

Project Editors: Kathleen Findorak, Lynn W. Kloss

Contributing Editor: Jacqueline M. Kiraithe-Córdova

Production Editor: June E. Bodansky

Art Director: Nancy Sharkey

Production Manager: Winston Sukhnanand

Desktop Specialist: José López

Cover Design: Richard Puder Design

Marketing Managers: Elmer Ildefonso, Sandra Hutchison

Manufacturing Coordinator: Lisa Cowart

Photo Research: Omni Photo Communications, Inc.

Cover: Estudiantes Leiendo (Students Reading), by Tony Ortega

Literature and art acknowledgments can be found on pages 152–154.

Printed in the United States of America.
 2 3 4 5 6 7 8 9 10 96 95 94 93

ISBN: 0-835-90539–X

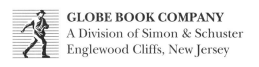

GLOBE BOOK COMPANY
A Division of Simon & Schuster
Englewood Cliffs, New Jersey

CONTENTS

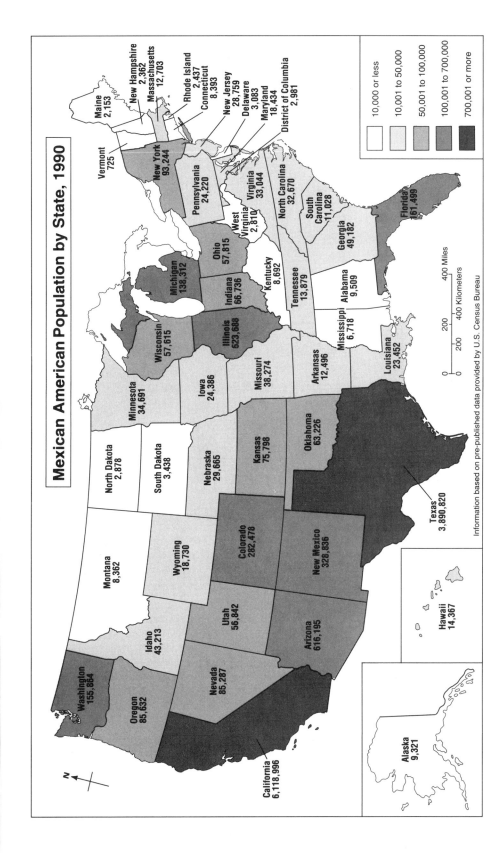

Mexican American Population by State, 1990

Legend:
- 10,000 or less
- 10,001 to 50,000
- 50,001 to 100,000
- 100,001 to 700,000
- 700,001 or more

Maine	2,153
New Hampshire	2,362
Massachusetts	12,703
Rhode Island	2,437
Connecticut	8,393
New Jersey	28,759
Delaware	3,083
Maryland	18,434
District of Columbia	2,981
Vermont	725
New York	93,244
Pennsylvania	24,220
West Virginia	2,810
Virginia	33,044
North Carolina	32,670
South Carolina	11,028
Florida	161,499
Georgia	49,182
Ohio	57,815
Kentucky	8,692
Tennessee	13,879
Alabama	9,509
Mississippi	6,718
Louisiana	23,452
Michigan	138,312
Indiana	66,736
Illinois	623,688
Wisconsin	57,615
Minnesota	34,691
Iowa	24,386
Missouri	38,274
Arkansas	12,496
North Dakota	2,878
South Dakota	3,438
Nebraska	29,665
Kansas	75,798
Oklahoma	63,226
Texas	3,890,820
Montana	8,362
Wyoming	18,730
Colorado	282,478
New Mexico	328,836
Idaho	43,213
Utah	56,842
Arizona	616,195
Washington	155,864
Oregon	85,632
Nevada	85,287
California	6,118,996
Hawaii	14,367
Alaska	9,321

400 Miles
400 Kilometers
0   200   400

N

Information based on pre-published data provided by U.S. Census Bureau

Titles of literature are placed in the time box to reflect, when possible, the historical time or event about which the selections are written.

1910–1920 Revolution in Mexico

1912 Arizona and New Mexico become states.

1917 Immigration Act of 1917 places head tax on Mexicans and other immigrants and requires proof of literacy.

Yo Soy Chicano ▼

Bailando ▼

1920s Southwestern states develop "Americanization" programs for newly arrived Mexicans.

1920–1929 Growers in Southwest recruit Mexican workers to meet growing demand for labor.

1933–1938 Mexican farm workers strike in California and Texas.

Recuerdo: How I changed the war and won the game. ▼

1941–1945 U.S. participation in World War II: 17 Mexican Americans win Congressional Medals of Honor for bravery.

An Interview with Tomás Rivera ▼

1942 United States and Mexico organize Bracero Program to set minimum wages and improve living and working conditions for Mexican workers.

My Father Is a Simple Man ▼

1945 California outlaws segregation of Mexican Americans in state-supported schools. Decision upheld by Supreme Court.

Freeway 280 ▼

My Wonder Horse ▼

1961 Henry B. Gonzalez of San Antonio, Texas, becomes first Mexican American to serve in U.S. House of Representatives.

And the Earth Did Not Devour Him ▼

1962 Cesar Chávez forms what later becomes United Farm Workers of America.

1964 Joseph Montoya of New Mexico becomes first Mexican American to serve in the U.S. Senate.

Nani ▼

1967 Federal Bilingual Act makes funds available for bilingual education programs.

1967–1968 First Mexican American Studies programs established in colleges and universities in Southwest.

My Name, Laughter, Four Skinny Trees, A Smart Cookie ▼

Old Man ▼

1970 U.S. Census reports Illinois has more Mexican immigrants than Arizona or New Mexico.

Señora X No More ▼

1971 Mexican American women hold first Chicana's Conference.

1974 Raul Castro becomes first Mexican American elected governor of Arizona.

Growing Up ▼

Picturesque: San Cristóbal de las Casas ▼

1980 U.S. Census reports about 85 percent of Mexican Americans live in cities.

The Flying Tortilla Man ▼

1980–1989 Spanish-language TV, newspapers, magazines, and radio stations spring up in United States.

1986 Congress passes Immigration Reform Act, offering amnesty to illegal aliens and allowing growers to import foreign farm workers.

DEAR STUDENT:

All the cultures that make up the United States have played a major part in molding the history of this country. In the following pages, you will read literature written by Mexican Americans. As you read the essays, stories, poems, interview, and play, reflect on the special traditions, beliefs, and heritages that are part of the Mexican American experience.

The literature is arranged into four units. Each unit represents a particular form of literature. The selections in the first unit are factual in nature and focus on personal experiences. The second unit consists of fictional stories based on the rich cultural roots of the authors. The third unit presents two groups of poems. In the first group, the poets make discoveries about themselves through their relationships with family members and respected adults. In the second group, the poets reflect on the people and places that inspired them. The fourth unit presents a drama that combines aspects of Mexican American culture with fantasy, realism, and humor.

In addition, the book features a map that shows how the Mexican American population is spread throughout the United States. A time box displays information about historical events that occurred during the period in which each selection is set.

As you read, think about the writing. The selections represent the experiences of many who came to this country in search of a better life. The literature of Mexican Americans reveals what makes their culture special, while bringing to light the commonality of all cultures.

UNIT 1

NONFICTION OF THE MEXICAN AMERICANS

Unlike fiction, which describes imaginary characters and events, nonfiction concentrates on real life. The characters are real people, the settings are real places, and the events actually happened.

There are many forms of nonfiction. Some nonfiction includes factual newspaper articles as well as the very personal stories that unfold in autobiographies, biographies, and interviews. Other forms of nonfiction include letters, diaries, journals, speeches, editorials, and essays. By combining facts with their personal feelings, opinions, and thoughts, nonfiction authors offer new and interesting ways to look at the world.

The first selection in this unit is an autobiographical account by David F. Gomez entitled "Yo Soy Chicano." In this piece, the author recalls his childhood struggles for acceptance by mainstream society. The next selection is an autobiographical essay by Mary Helen Ponce entitled "Recuerdo: How I changed the war and won the game." Written from the perspective of an 8-year-old girl, the essay recounts one of Ponce's humorous childhood experiences. In the last selection, Tomás Rivera is interviewed by Juan Bruce-Novoa. In the interview, Rivera answers questions about his family history, his experiences as a migrant farmer, and his formal education. As you read these selections, think about how the authors reveal their thoughts and opinions through descriptions of real events and situations.

Tamalada. (Tamale-Making.) Gouache painting by Chicana artist Carmen Lomas Garza. Garza often portrays family gatherings and other celebrations of Chicano society. These images contrast with the poverty and discrimination she faced growing up in a small Texas town.

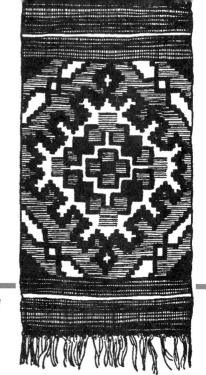

INTRODUCTION
Yo Soy Chicano
(I Am Chicano)

The son of Mexican immigrants, David F. Gomez was born in California in 1940. Both his parents had come as teenagers to the United States. With their families, they hoped to find a better life. A revolution that swept through Mexico in 1910 had made life there dangerous and left many without jobs or food. With little formal education, Gomez's parents learned to speak English without an accent and quickly adapted to mainstream society. Gomez was raised in a mostly white, lower-middle-class neighborhood in southwest Los Angeles. Although he and his family made many trips to Mexico during his childhood, Gomez proudly considered himself "American."

It was not until he entered school that Gomez realized that mainstream society considered him inferior. Accepting mainstream standards, Gomez gave up his Mexican heritage. Yet he felt like an outsider among his white classmates and teachers. The selection you are about to read, "Yo Soy Chicano," is from Gomez's book *Somos Chicanos: Strangers in Our Own Land*. In this autobiographical account, Gomez discusses the difficulties that arise from being caught between two cultures and feeling like an outsider in both.

Yo Soy Chicano (I Am Chicano)

by David F. Gomez

II

Through brown eyes, seeing only brown colors and feeling only
    brown feelings . . . I saw . . . I felt . . . I hated . . . I cried . . . I tried.

. . .

While, on the side . . . I realized I BELIEVED in
white as pretty,
    my being governor,
        blonde blue eyed baby Jesus,
            cokes and hamburgers,
                equality for all regardless of race, creed, or
                    color,
                Mr. Williams, our banker.
I had to!
That was all I had.
Beans and Communism were bad.

—JOSE ANGEL GUTIERREZ[1]

MY EARLY SCHOOLING was a terribly destructive experience, for it stripped away my identity as a *Mexicano*

---

1. **Jose Angel Gutierrez** (hoh-SAY AHN-hel goo-tee-AIR-ays)

and alienated me from my own people, including my parents. At the age of six I entered Seventy-fifth Street School, which was located down the street we lived on. The school was predominantly white, at least 85 percent or more. The rest of us were either Mexican, black, or Oriental, but mostly Mexican. The teachers in the school were white, and for the next twelve years I never encountered a nonwhite teacher in the system. In the classroom my most vivid memories are those of Dick, Jane, and Spot in the first- and second-grade readers. Dick and Jane, of course, were white children, and even their dog Spot looked white and clean. Everything that was of value or importance in school was white and clean. The teachers either ignored our Mexican heritage completely or referred to us condescendingly as "Spanish." At first it annoyed me to be called Spanish because Papá had strictly taught us to say, *"Soy puro Mexicano"* ("I am 100 percent Mexican!") when asked what we were. The white teachers obviously knew what we were but, filled with good intentions, probably wanted to soften the ugly sound of "Mexican" by calling us Spanish. On the playground, of course, it was a different matter. The white children called us "dirty Mexicans" (that's why our skin was brown) or cowards who ran from fights (like our ancestors at the Alamo).[2] My predominant impression, therefore, was the Mexicans had no legitimate place in the white world. If we Mexicans wanted to survive at all, we would have to become white. And I wanted to be white.

My mother came to visit me only once in school. It was during my year in the third grade. Mamá said that after school let out she would take me shopping with her. I expected to find her waiting in the car out front as she usually did when she picked me up, but instead she parked

---

2. **the Alamo** (AH-lah-moh) a mission in San Antonio, Texas; scene of a massacre of Texans by Mexican troops in 1836

the car and came into the building to get me. By the time she got upstairs to the classroom it was 2:00 P.M. and the last bell had rung. Most of the other children were putting away their books and papers, getting their coats and sweaters from the cloakroom, or huddling around the teacher's desk. Everyone seemed to be talking very loud or laughing—as only children can do when the school day has ended. My mother entered the classroom through the front door, and when she saw me she called out, *"David, apúrate, te 'stoy esperando!"*[3] I froze with embarrassment and shame, feeling that everyone in the room was staring at us. And I didn't want the other children to think of me as different or foreign. I ran up to my mother and pleaded, "Mother, speak *English* please!" She never mentioned the incident, but I know I must have disappointed her.

My parents kept close contact with the land of their birth. It is about 140 miles from Los Angeles to Tijuana, and about 200 miles to Mexicali. Many of my relatives would head south across the border to have dental or medical work done. They went not only because the work could be done less expensively but also because they would be better able to communicate with the doctor in their own language. My parents did not have any language problems, but we would head south anyway just for the recreation and the opportunity to visit with friends and relatives there. My brother's *padrinos* (godparents) lived there, and that was a special relationship that linked our families closely together. Each summer my sister and I would swim in the *arroyito*[4] with local Mexican children and enjoy ourselves, but later it seemed that we enjoyed ourselves just as much at home. Besides I didn't like

---

3. *"Davíd, apúrate, te 'stoy esperando!"* (dah-VEED, ah-POO-rah-tay, tay stoi ays-pay-RAHN-doh) David, hurry up, I'm waiting for you

4. *arroyito* (ahr-roy-EE-toh) *n.* small stream

the steady diet of beans and tortillas that our hosts served with every meal. Back home we had beans and tortillas with supper only, but in Agua Caliente[5] we had it with every meal.

Gradually I became aware of feeling that what my family had to offer—language, customs, food, ways of looking at the world, vacations in Baja California—was not very good in comparison with the other world in which I lived. This was the world of little Richard Yates, Donald Cook, Patricia Allen, and the other white kids who went to Seventy-fifth Street School with me. I went out of my way as much as possible to get into their world.

My early childhood playmates, other than my own relatives, were white children, and I preferred their companionship to that of my own people. There was one little boy (whose name I've since forgotten) who was in the third grade with me. I wanted him to be my friend because he seemed to embody all that I admired and believed was best. He had blond hair, bright blue eyes, and rosy cheeks. In fact, he looked a lot like Dick, the little *gringo*[6] hero in our first- and second-grade readers. And I was determined to make friends with him. On the playground during recess, I went up to him and offered him the supreme sacrifice I was capable of offering, my leather pouch, a valuable little pouch made of soft leather which I had saved box tops for months to finally get. You could wear the pouch on your belt and carry a lot of marbles or candy in it. "Here," I said to the little blond boy, holding up the pouch so he could take it, "do you want it?" "Yeah . . . don't you need it?" He seemed more puzzled than

---

5. **Agua Caliente** (AH-gwah kah-lee-AYN-tay) a small state in the center of Mexico
6. *gringo* (GREEN-goh) *adj.* slang term for someone from the United States

gratified by my generosity. I told him I didn't need it anymore and he could have it. So he took my pouch—but not my friendship—and went off to play in another corner of the playground with his own friends. Perhaps I somehow knew all along that I couldn't buy his friendship and that all I would succeed in doing would be to pay homage[7] to the symbol of what I most admired and wanted to be.

Our principal at Seventy-fifth Street School was an elderly, soft-spoken lady with silver-white hair and an unctuous[8] but dignified smile. At assemblies she led us through the flag-raising ritual, pledge of allegiance, and the morning prayer. Naturally, Miss Kelly impressed me as a very fine, religiously sensitive person. At least she did until the day I was called into her office. No one had told me what it was all about, and I was nervous as the secretary ushered me into Miss Kelly's office. It was a stern, almost severe office with a large reproduction of Gilbert Stuart's George Washington—the kind one sees in most public schools—hanging from the wall. She sat beneath the portrait and behind the largest desk I had ever seen. I stood there terrified by her presence but also curiously fascinated by how much Miss Kelly and George Washington looked alike. They even had the same phony smile.

But Miss Kelly wasn't smiling this time. "We know," she said in a deliberately harsh voice that quivered with indignation, "we know for a fact that you have been playing with a knife on the playground. And don't try to deny it because people have seen you!" I didn't try to deny anything because I was too scared and too numb to protest my innocence. I only knew that everything she was saying

---

7. **pay homage** (PAY HAHM-ihj) to show honor or respect
8. **unctuous** (UNK-choo-uhs) *adj.* smug; greasy or oily in manner

about me was completely untrue. So I stood there, knees shaking and completely defenseless before my judge and jury—condemned by Miss Kelly and George Washington! After pronouncing me guilty, she dismissed me with a final warning. "We don't want people like you playing with the other children. If I don't have that knife soon, I'm going to call your parents and have them come in." For a long time after, I was in a state of shock. How could anyone be so wrong about me? Days passed, and nothing happened. Later on, another student who heard it from someone else told me the whole thing had been a case of mistaken identity. Another Mexican boy named Michael Moreno had scared some of the small children with his pocket knife, and the principal had gotten the wrong Mexican—me.

Like many Mexican American children my school experiences made a peripheral[9] person of me. My Anglo–white experiences at school so completely conflicted with my Mexican–brown experiences at home that I rejected one for the other only to find that I couldn't fully participate in either. I became a withdrawn person living on the periphery of the white world and wanting to have less and less to do with the brown world. And having been taught Mexican good manners at home I waited to be invited into the white world which I saw as all-important and superior to my brown world. But no one in the white world would invite me in. I should have realized that the Anglo-white promise of acceptance and equality was a total lie and a double-cross, but still I held out hope. So I waited and waited, and gradually waiting became a way of existence—existing in neither the white world nor the brown. I was indeed a "Mexican American," a hyphenated person who

---

9. **peripheral** (puh-RIHF-uhr-uhl) *adj.* on the edge; outside of the center

was somehow both Mexican and American yet neither a Mexican nor an American in any clearly defined sense.

Sometimes when the brown world intruded into the white, I felt divided within myself, but usually I ended up choosing the white world. Most of the time, I was simply a displaced person who, in his better moments, should have realized he was trying to be someone or something he actually was not. I believed that I was white, a belief that left permanent scars on my consciousness because it uprooted me from my *familia* and created in me the false and deceptive impression that I was really accepted and belonged in the white world. All the while I believed or wanted to believe I could be accepted by whites, the real way in which white society perceived me was being permanently carved into my personality. I wasn't an equal but only a weak and inferior being. (Close friends have confided to me that the first impression I gave them was one of *weakness*. The way I spoke to them and looked made them think I was weak. Only after getting to know me were they able to see that despite this appearance, I was not like that at all.) I gave many people the impression of being weak because I have been a marginal, peripheral person in a dominant society for so long that unconsciously I assumed all the characteristics that the dominant group expected of me.

Being a *Mexicano* in Anglo-land caused me the most frustration and pain during junior and senior high school. When I entered John Muir Junior High I began to take an active interest in girls, which was natural enough for a thirteen-year-old boy. But the only feminine beauty I had been conditioned to see was white. Rosalind Russell, Jean Simmons, and Doris Day were my movie favorites. What I saw on television or in magazine pictures only reinforced my conviction that the only beautiful women or girls were white. I found myself staring at and wanting to touch *gringitas.*[10] There were also many Mexican girls in school, but if they did not look like *gringas* I didn't feel they were attractive. The white standard of beauty affected my little cousin María in an especially tragic way. She was in grammar school at this time, and I remember her as being small for her age with large, dark eyes, long, shiny black hair, and a very swarthy complexion. Years later, María bitterly recalled her childhood and how her mother often powdered her face to make the little girl look less like a dark *Mexicana* and more white. Thus she would be more acceptable to white society and, by obvious implication, to her mother as well. To most Mexicans, swarthiness is a sign of beauty, but to many of us who were caught up in the values of the dominant society, it was only a badge of inferiority. For that reason I should have realized that the little *gringas* were as far beyond my reach as the movie stars I gaped at. The very standard that made them so attractive to me also made me ultimately unacceptable to them.

At school I played alongside tough Mexican boys from the *barrios*. They wore their clothes in *pachuco*[11] style, wearing their Levis and khaki trousers low with unbuttoned sports shirts outside the trousers. They combed their hair in a ducktail (a style they had originated) and wore dark sunglasses both indoors and outside—even if the sun was not out. They were *vatos locos,*[12] always fighting with the *mayates*[13] or *gringos* or, if no one else was around, they would fight among themselves. They were as tough as young men come; and as a sign of how mean they were they wore small cross-shaped tattoos

---

10. *gringitas* (green-GEE-tas) *n. pl.* (slang) little American girls
11. *pachuco* (pah-CHOO-koh) *adj.* (slang) Mexican American gang member
12. *vatos locos* (VAH-tohs LOH-kohs) *n. pl.* (slang) crazy guys
13. *mayates* (may-YAH-tays) *n. pl.* slang term for African Americans

on the backs of their hands where the thumb and index finger meet. Their *placas* (names of *barrios* or gangs) were distinctively drawn in Chicano script on sidewalks, school walls, or any wall or surface they could reach with an aerosol spray can or magic marker without being caught by the police. One of the *vatos*, Ricardo, tried to befriend me. He had noticed how I dressed and spoke (more like the *gringos* I was imitating than a Chicano) and approached me between classes to ask me about it. "Hey, *ese*,[14] aren't you a Mexican? You don't talk like one. . . ." "Yes, I'm a Mexican," I answered defensively, trying to avert his look. He was only trying to be a friend in setting me straight, but from then on I avoided him whenever I could.

Later there were times when I looked back and wished that I'd become one of the *locos*. At first I thought they were unashamed to be Mexicans, unashamed to proudly assert the very differences the rest of us sought to deny, conceal, or powder over. But I now realize that I had more in common with the *vatos locos* than I knew at the time. We were actually in the same situation. No longer Mexicans and denied the full status of white Americans, we were only doing our best to be somebody. We were trying to define our identities as best we knew how. The *vatos* wrote their names on walls and made obscene gestures at The Establishment[15] as if to say they knew who they were and didn't need anyone else. On the other hand, I was trying to crash the gates of *gringo*-land, believing that I would be who I wanted to be once I got in.

When I entered John C. Fremont High my best friend was Leo Garcia. He was a big Chicano, standing about six

---

14. *ese* (AY-say) *n.* (slang) man (you)
15. **The Establishment** (uh-STAB-lihsh-muhnt) the ruling circle of any group or nation

feet tall with a handsome face and very dark coloring. I owe a great deal to Leo, for he did what the school had been unwilling and unable to do. Leo convinced me that I had the ability to succeed in my studies and persuaded me to take college preparatory courses in high school. Leo had a good mind and saw the importance of learning. He would astound everyone by reciting from memory the batting averages and other lifetime statistics of Babe Ruth, Ty Cobb, and other baseball greats. He took me under his wing, and I developed a real interest in reading and doing well in class. I had planned to take a trade school course like auto mechanics, which all the Chicanos and blacks had been counseled to take. But Leo convinced me that it would be better to prepare for college and the better jobs available to college graduates. The courses were harder than I expected, but gradually I improved. Besides, I was so well-behaved and stood in such contrast with the troublesome *vatos* and blacks that my teachers rewarded me with good grades.

During our high school days Leo and I had several run-ins with the law. As far as I could tell the only reason the Los Angeles Police Department had for picking us up so often was that we were Mexicans and to them Mexicans were more likely to be *marijuanitos* (dope addicts) than anyone else. The first time it happened was the most memorable, perhaps because it was the first. On a Saturday evening in the fall of our freshman year, Leo and I were walking home after playing baseball in the park. We had played hard all afternoon until it was so dark we couldn't see the ball anymore. As we walked along Vermont Avenue, not far from Slauson, Leo carried most of the playing equipment in a canvas athletic bag while I carried the bat over my shoulder. From out of nowhere an unmarked police car pulled alongside of us and came to a halt. Two plainclothes detectives got out of the car and ordered us to drop what we had in our hands and roll up our shirt sleeves. When they didn't find any needle marks they started questioning me about the "menacing" way I'd been "brandishing" the bat. Leo didn't like the rough treatment and antagonized them by answering their questions in the same belligerent tone of voice in which they were being asked. In response the police put us both in the patrol car and took us to the local station. They took Leo into a separate room and tried to break his spirit by browbeating[16] him for at least an hour, but he didn't give in. Meanwhile, they had decided that I was a *good* Mexican because I had not talked back to them or questioned their authority (actually I was scared speechless). But they called Leo "stupid" because he didn't know how to "keep his big mouth shut." Then they let us go because we had not done anything. That was the first of many such experiences.

Although the police may not have thought so, Leo and I were very much alike. We were equally attracted to the other world which good grades and high school honors promised us. By the time I graduated from high school I had applied to and been accepted by Loyola University in Los Angeles, and Leo was planning to attend Los Angeles City College. My first day at Loyola was a frightening experience. This was not due merely to my having to travel to an unfamiliar part of town for the first time or face the totally different world of the college campus by myself. I was terrified because never before had I seen so many white people of college and adult age all together at the same time. In high school my classmates were either Chicanos or blacks, and the last time I had been in a predominantly white school was my last year in junior high school. At Loyola, I felt like a foreigner in a strange land. One of the things that struck me so forcefully

---

16. **browbeating** (BROW-beet-ihng) *v.* bullying with harsh looks and talk

at the time was that the white fellows, most of whom were seventeen or eighteen years old, looked as if they had to shave every morning, something many Chicanos and blacks like myself found unnecessary. It made me feel like a mere boy among grown men.

That first afternoon at Loyola, I found that the feeling of alienation was not just a product of my imagination. Those same people who so terrified me by their whiteness and made me feel out of place actually considered me an alien. In order to register for courses we had to sign up for them with individual registrars who checked our registration materials and made sure we were eligible to take the course. All freshmen were required to take a foreign language, and I chose Spanish. I got into the line for the Spanish courses, but when my turn came and I gave the registrar my registration cards, she looked at the name on the cards and then looked at me and exclaimed, "You can't take your own language!" She strongly suggested that I should concentrate on mastering English first. I was so overcome with confusion that I simply turned away and went to the back of another line. That semester I ended up taking beginner's French.

In my first year of college I wanted to be a part of the white world so badly that I did something I regretted for a long time after. I enlisted in the Marine Corps Officer Training Program. Of all things, a recruiter poster in front of a post office attracted me. It pictured a Nordic-looking, strong, and independent *Macho*. If being a Marine had done that for him maybe it could do the same for me—or so I thought. Like so many Chicanos who join the Marines, I was prompted to join up because of my sense of *machismo*.[17] After all, our only image of manliness was what we saw on television and in the movies: John Wayne

---

17. *machismo* (mah-CHEES-moh) *n.* aggressive masculinity

fighting for America's freedom at Iwo Jima or the Alamo. But for me there was more: I believed that by becoming a Marine officer I would at last find acceptance. If only I could wear the Marine uniform people would forget what I wanted to forget more than anything else: my dark skin, coarse black hair, and Spanish surname. It didn't work out that way because after six weeks of summer training I couldn't pass the written tests and was flunked out of the program. My heart wasn't in the program, and in that sense my failure was a fitting end to something I should never have attempted to be: a white *Macho* whom other whites would accept and admire.

I never told my parents about my failure because I didn't want them to be ashamed of me. While they naturally would have been disappointed, they would have shown me the same *cariño*[18] I had always experienced within the *familia.* But the world of Anglo values which stressed success and frowned on failure dominated my actions. I was cut off from my parents in a more profound way than just the generation gap. I was also cut off from my Mexican roots. Nor was I able to look to Leo for friendship or emotional support. He had dropped out of college after the second year, and that, coupled with his being a Mexican (a mirror image of the identity I had tried to put behind me) led me to have less and less to do with him until we were no longer friends. Leo was the only Chicano I knew who had gotten as far as college with me (a remarkable achievement for Chicanos!), and it seemed almost natural for him, as a Chicano with his roots still in the *familia,* to drop out. He was also the last Chicano I would have as a real friend for many years to come. At least in the way I treated Leo, I had indeed become the *gabacho*[19] I so desperately wanted to be.

---

18. *cariño* (kah-REEN-nyoh) *n.* affection
19. *gabacho* (gah-BAH-choh) *n.* gringo, European-American

AFTER YOU READ

Exchanging Backgrounds and Cultures

1. How do Gomez's attitudes toward his heritage change when he enters school? Give examples.
2. Which events in Gomez's life best represent the discrimination and injustice Mexican Americans confront?
3. How do Gomez's experiences in school make him feel that he does not fit into either the Mexican or mainstream world?

What Do You Think?

Which person or event in this autobiographical sketch is most meaningful to you? Why?

Experiencing Nonfiction

In this sketch, Gomez describes the events in his childhood that made him question his identity. Which events in your life have made you wonder about your role or place in society? How did these same events help you grow as a person? Write an autobiographical sketch that discusses an experience that made you question your identity.

Optional Activity Write an autobiographical sketch that describes a special person who has changed or shaped your values. For instance, in Gomez's autobiographical account, he talks about how his relationship with Leo made him study more and work harder.

INTRODUCTION

Recuerdo: How I changed the war and won the game.

Born in 1938, Mary Helen Ponce grew up in a large Mexican American family. She was raised in a small barrio, or Hispanic neighborhood, in Pacoima, California. As a child, Ponce loved to read. By reading about other people's lives, she realized that her own personal stories were also worth writing down. Ponce believes that growing up in the barrio has made her more sensitive to those who have difficulty adjusting to the language and customs of a new country. Her writing often reflects her awareness of the immigrant experience and her strong ties to her Hispanic heritage.

Inspired by the Chicano movement, the Mexican American civil rights movement that developed in the 1960s, Ponce majored in Mexican American studies in college and began to take an interest in Latin American literature. The following autobiographical essay is a *recuerdo,* or remembrance, in which Ponce recounts a humorous childhood experience.

Recuerdo: How I changed the war and won the game.

by Mary Helen Ponce

During World War II, I used to translate the English newspaper's war news for our adopted grandmother Doña[1] Luisa and her friends. All of them were *señoras de edad,*[2] elderly ladies who could not read English, only their native Spanish.

Every afternoon they would gather on Doña Luisa's front porch to await Doña Trinidad's son who delivered the paper to her promptly at 5 P.M. There, among the *geranios*[3] and pots of *yerba buena*[4] I would bring them the news of the war.

At first I enjoyed doing this, for the *señoras* would welcome me as a grown-up. They would push their chairs around in a semicircle, the better to hear me. I would sit in the middle, on a *banquito*[5] that was a milk crate. I don't remember how I began to be their translator but because I

1. **Doña** (DOHN-nyah) *n.* title of respect used before first names of women, like Ma'am
2. *señoras de edad* (say-NYOR-ahs day ay-DAHD) elderly ladies
3. *geranios* (hay-RAH-nee-ohs) *n. pl.* geraniums, a kind of flower
4. *yerba buena* (YAIR-bah BWAY-nah) mint (tea)
5. *banquito* (bahn-KEE-toh) *n.* little bench

was an obedient child and at eight a good reader, I was somehow coerced or selected.

I would sit down, adjust my dress, then slowly unwrap the paper, reading the headlines to myself in English, trying to decide which news items were the most important, which to tell first. Once I had decided, I would translate them into my best Spanish for Doña Luisa and her friends.

The news of a battle would bring sighs of *Jesús, María y José, Ay Dios Mío,*[6] from the ladies. They would roll their eyes toward heaven, imploring our Lord to protect their loved ones from danger. In return they vowed to light candles or to make a *manda,*[7] a pilgrimage to *la Virgen de San Juan*[8] in the nearby town of Sunland. Once I had read them the highlights of the war I was allowed to play ball with my friends.

One day we had an important ball game going, our team was losing, and it was my turn at bat. Just then Doña Luisa called me. It was time for *las noticias.*[9] Furious at this interruption yet not daring to disobey, I dropped the bat, ran to the porch, ripped open the paper, pointed to the headlines and in a loud voice proclaimed: "Ya están los japoneses en San Francisco . . . los esperan en Los Angeles muy pronto,"[10] or "The Japanese have landed in San Francisco; they should be in Los Angeles soon."

---

6. *Jesús, María y José, Ay Dios Mío* (hay-SOOS mah-REE-yah EE hoh-SAY eye DEE-yohs MEE-yoh) Jesus, Mary and Joseph, oh dear God

7. *manda* (MAHN-dah) *n.* a vow

8. *la Virgen de San Juan* (lah VEER-hen day sahn WHAN) the Virgin of San Juan

9. *las noticas* (lahs noh-TEE-see-ahs) the news

10. **Ya están los japoneses en San Francisco . . . los esperan en Los Angeles muy pronto** (YAH ays-TAHN lohs ha-poh-NAY-says ayn sahn frahn-SEES-koh . . . lohs ays-PAY-rahn ayn lohs AHN-hay-lays moo-ee PROHN-toh)

"Jesús, María y José, Sangre de Cristo, Ave María, Purísima"[11] chanted las señoras as I dashed off to resume my game. *"Dios mío ya vámonos, ya vámonos"*[12] they said as chairs were pushed aside, *"vamos a la Iglesia . . . a rezarle al Señor."*[13]

After that I was able to translate according to whim—and depending on whether or not I was up to bat when the paper arrived.

---

11. *Sangre de Cristo, Ave María, Purísima* (SAHN-gray day KREES-toh AH-vay mah-REE-yah poo-REE-see-mah) These are exclamations similar to *blood of Christ* and *hail Mary, most pure.*
12. *Dios mío ya vámonos, ya vámonos* (DEE-yohs MEE-yoh YAH VAH-moh-nohs, YAH VAH-moh-nohs) My God, we're going, we're going.
13. *vamos a la Iglesia . . . a rezarle al Señor* (VAH-mohs ah lah ee-GLAY-see-yah . . . ah ray-SAHR-lay ahl sayn-NYOHR) Let's go to church . . . to pray to the Lord.

AFTER YOU READ

Exchanging Backgrounds and Cultures

1. How do Ponce's feelings about the war differ from that of the older women? Why do you think their feelings are so different?

2. How does Ponce show her maturity in the beginning of the essay? How does she show that she is only a child at the end of the sketch?

3. What do the older women do when they hear the headlines? What does this reveal about traditional Mexican American culture?

What Do You Think?

Which part of this sketch is especially meaningful to you? Why is it important?

Experiencing Nonfiction

In her autobiographical essay, Ponce shows what she thinks as a child and shows the humor of the incident. Think about something funny in your life that seemed important or serious at the time. Then, write an essay that describes the event and shows that your attitude about it has changed over time.

Optional Activity Write a personal account of your relationship to an older friend or relative. Like Ponce, who reveals that translating to the older women made her feel grown-up, describe how your role in the relationship affects your sense of identity.

INTRODUCTION

An Interview with Tomás Rivera

Juan Bruce-Novoa is a recognized writer, critic, commentator, and teacher of Mexican American literature. Born in 1944, he grew up in Denver, Colorado, surrounded by a family of writers, musicians, and painters. As a child in elementary school, he began writing short stories. As a young adult, he became a rock-and-blues musician. He continued working as a musician while in college, graduating in 1966 with a degree in history.

Bruce-Novoa went on to get his doctorate in Contemporary Mexican Literature in 1974. He then turned to teaching and writing. A professor of Chicano and Mexican Literature at Yale University, Bruce-Novoa has published many short stories, poems, and critical reviews of the works of Mexican American authors. The book of interviews, from which the following excerpt was taken, came about when Bruce-Novoa discovered that there were no source materials on Mexican American authors. He sought out 14 leading contemporary Chicano writers and asked them questions about family life, culture, education, and literature. Tomás Rivera, one of these distinguished fiction writers, reveals his experiences and feelings.

An Interview with Tomás Rivera

by Juan Bruce-Novoa

Tomás Rivera's responses were recorded in San Antonio, Texas, in June 1977, and he reviewed the text in September 1979.

When and where were you born?

December 22, 1935, in Crystal City, Texas, which is about 120 miles southwest of here [San Antonio].

Describe your family background and your present situation.

My parents were born in Mexico, my mother in Coahuila[1] and my father in Aguascalientes.[2] He came to the United States at an early age, about fifteen, and wandered into El Paso, then up to the Midwest, and worked mostly on the railroad, as a cook in different places. In 1930, on his way back to Mexico, he arrived in Crystal City, where he met my mother and they got married. My mother's family also came to the states soon after she was born, around 1920,

---

1. **Coahuila** (koh-ah-HWEE-lah) *n.* a state in northern Mexico, next to Texas
2. **Aguascalientes** (AH-gwahs-kah-lee-AYN-tays) *n.* a small state in the center of Mexico

traveling up to Dallas, then to Houston, then back to Austin for a while, until around 1930 they ended up in Crystal City.

Crystal City was at the time and is still called the Winter Garden area. In the 1920's the city became a center for truck farming, mostly for vegetables that could be grown in the winter and shipped to San Antonio. It's a fairly new town, incorporated in 1922, and it attracted many immigrants from Mexico, because it was on the route to San Antonio. So my grandparents on my mother's side settled there.

They had come first to Eagle Pass, right across the river from Piedras Negras, where my mother attended the American public school for a couple of years. She learned to read and write in a rural school in Las Minas del Seco.

My grandfather had been in mining in northern Mexico, involved in the union organization of the minas del norte de Coahuila [mines of northern Coahuila]. During the Revolution[3] he had been an officer. I didn't know this until just before he died he told me. As I had grown older I began to notice that he knew a lot of things, especially about the war, the war theatres, movement of troops, logistics, and so forth, and military history in general; he knew all of it very well. Before he died he had a cerebral attack which left him crippled. I was talking to him one time about the Civil War in the United States and he began to explain certain things about it; so I asked him where he had learned them, because he had no education in this country, though he had learned to read and write English when he came here. He replied, "Well, I'll tell you, I've really lived two

---

3. **Revolution** (rev-uh-LOO-shuhn) the Mexican Revolution, which overthrew dictator Porfirio Díaz

lives, one in Mexico and another here. In Mexico I grew up as a peón[4] in an hacienda,[5] but I became a very close friend of the son of the hacendado [hacienda owner], and when he wanted to send his son to military school, the son refused to go unless I went along; so the hacendado sent us both al Colegio Militar de México [to the Mexico Military Academy]." There he became an officer in the Federal Army. But later he fled the Revolución when he decided he didn't want any part of it any more. I knew none of this until he was dying, because he had had another family in Mexico y luego se había venido al norte y se había casado otra vez y tenía otra familia con otra señora [and then he had come to the north and had married again and had another family with another woman]. And he said he had studied military history at the military academy. Then I understood why he knew so much about all these things. He had never revealed any of that, not even to his sons and daughters, pero a mí sí me lo reveló [but he revealed it to me]. Anyway, the family ended up in Crystal City in 1930.

My father had no formal education, nor did my mother, except for the two years in public school. My dad knew how to read and write in Spanish and he could speak English.

We were migrant workers. By the time I was born, 1935, my grandfather's younger sons and daughters were old enough to participate in the migrant stream, so they wandered all over Texas. As early as 1934 they went north

---

4. **peón** (pay-OHN) *n.* worker
5. **hacienda** (ah-see-AYN-dah) *n.* a farm or ranch

to Michigan and Minnesota to the beet fields. That, more or less, is the background of the family as far as the economic base of working as farm laborers in Texas or the northern states.

My earliest recollections are of living on different farms where we worked in Minnesota. We used to go every year. The last year I worked as a migrant was 1956, when I was already in junior college. My parents were still working in Iowa, but I would only work three months and then I had to return to complete the year at the college. Through high school it was different: we would leave around April 15, and return around November 1; that was the working season. In the fall I'd finish the year before and start the next at the same time. At the high school level it was O.K., because it's easy to catch up, but the junior college wouldn't allow late registration, so I had to come home in early September. By my junior year I stopped going altogether; I had another job by then. My parents, however, were still going out.

Now I'm married and have three children. I am the vice president for administration at UTSA [University of Texas at San Antonio. Since the interview, Rivera has become the Chancellor of the University of California, Riverside, after a brief term as executive vice president at the University of Texas at El Paso.]

When did you first begin to write?

Creative writing? About eleven or twelve years old. That's when I first said, "I'm going to write a story and this is the title," and all that. We had had an accident and I wanted to write about it, so I called it "The Accident." I felt a sensation I still get when I write. I wanted to capture something I would never forget and it happened to be the sensation of having a wreck. I had never been involved in a wreck before, so I thought I had to get it down, because I felt no one had ever had a wreck like that and people should know about it. I wrote it down and it was crummy, real bad; but at the time I thought I had a winner: "The Accident." It happened in Bay City, Michigan.

It turned me on and I kept writing. I guess I wanted to write because by then I had been reading quite a bit. A voracious reader. Then I wanted to be a sportswriter. In high school I did a lot of writing, both essays and creative stuff, and published here and there. But I started around eleven and I really wanted to be a sportswriter. When people asked what I wanted to be, I'd tell them a writer. They were surprised or indifferent. If people don't read, what is a writer? No big thing; no one was impressed. Except my grandfather. I remember that.

My grandfather said that writing and art were the most important things, that to be a pintor, como decía él [painter, as he said], was an accomplishment. I was drawing a great deal at the time, and he encouraged me, buying me many materials to use, like all types of tablets. He showed me a little about drawing techniques. He could draw very well. I still have some of the drawings from when I was seven or eight.

I kept painting for a long time, until I got married, when I stopped. The first two years of our marriage my wife and I painted together. We lived in Crystal City, and there's not much to do there, so we would spend days painting, just painting, whole weekends. It passed the time and we found it a great way to be together. But then our first child came along y ya no hay lugar [and there's no place] nor time; then the second and you kind of put it aside. Maybe someday, when our kids are grown, we'll come back to it. We found it a very enjoyable experience. It takes all your energy and time; it's exhilarating. My grandfather was more enthused about art than writing.

What kind of books did you read in your formative years?

Two types: one, the sports stories and books; two, any kind of adventure story.

In Hampton, Iowa, there was a little old lady, tennis shoes and all, who helped me out. Every day I'd walk down to pick up the mail at the post office for my parents and pass the Carnegie Library. I didn't even know what . . . it meant; CARNEGIE; they were just letters to me. I was about ten years old and it was the first time I had come in contact with a library. This lady must have noticed me passing every day, so she stopped me one day and invited me in. She opened up a lot of things to me. She took me down into the basement and showed me all the periodicals. She'd ask me, "What do you want to know about?" This or that, I'd answer, and she would take out the newspaper where we could find it. Then she'd say, "Let's go back to 1900," and she'd take out a newspaper from 1900. Amazing, discovering all these things from the past right there and being able to read about them. Then she would say, "Here, you can take these books with you. Read them. Whenever you finish, return them." I couldn't believe it. Every day she had different readings for me, one or two books she thought I'd like; lots of sports books, especially. Then she introduced me to the mystery-type books. Y así iba dándome todo eso. [And in that way she gave me all that. Every summer we spent in Hampton, Iowa, I looked forward to going back to that library where she was waiting for me with all those books. I don't even remember her name.

My dad knew I liked to read, so he would go knocking on doors, asking if they had any old magazines, which he then brought home to me. We always had a lot of reading materials of all kinds. We also used to go to the dump to collect reading materials. I found encyclopedias and different types of books. At home I still have my dump collection gathered from the dumps in northern towns. People threw away a lot of books.

Encyclopedias fascinated me, because you could just read one thing after another. I find the same thing with my youngest kid, who is eleven. I bought him an encyclopedia three years ago and he's fascinated with it, because he can take any book, read from page to page finding out about one item after another, continually discovering things. I did the same thing years ago with old encyclopedias that people had thrown away.

There is one book which especially impressed me: *In Darkest Africa* by Henry M. Stanley. I found it myself in the dump, you see; a two-volume collection of Stanley's expedition[6] into Africa in search of Dr. Livingstone. Of course, I didn't know anything about history at the time, or the exploration of Africa, but with the books came maps of the terrain through which Stanley had to travel. The text was a diary, a day-by-day account of what to Stanley was the discovery of Africa, with all the details, like how much food they ate, how far they had traveled, all those things. It fascinated me. It was better than going to a Tarzan movie. It carried over into my own life, because I started making maps of the terrain we traveled, and my brothers and I would explore and draw maps. It became a living thing. I haven't read them for a long time, but that title stuck in my memory because of the exploratory aspect. Later, when I ran into other similar things, I was able to understand the

---

6. **Stanley's expedition** Dr. David Livingstone was a Scottish physician, missionary, and explorer. In 1869, Sir Henry M. Stanley was sent to Africa to find the missing Dr. Livingstone, who had not been heard from for several years. Stanley found Livingstone on November 10, 1871.

exploration of America and Latin America because I could understand this one man's exploration of the Dark Continent. I still have those books at home.

That was back in 1944; I was about nine, but I could understand it pretty well. I reread that book. I would read chapters to my mother or to my dad, and they liked it too. The Tarzan movies came on pretty strong around then, with the serials every Saturday, but to me they were already fake. Henry M. Stanley was the real thing.

Another thing about those books that fascinated me was that they had been published in the 1880's, and they were still in good shape when I found them, though they must have been fifty or so years old. I don't know what happened to the maps; maybe they fell out. See, the maps fit into pockets, so they could be spread out and you could follow the journey. I might have lost them because I carried them with me to Iowa or Minnesota. I don't know how I would react to them now, but it's the first title I remember, *In Darkest Africa.*

There were other titles, like *The Last Backboard,* and *The Last Touchdown,* or *Iron Fist.* All the stuff you read when you are eight years old. The *Wizard of Oz* fascinated me when I first read it.

Junior high school was lost; no reading that was worthwhile, pure mishmash. First of all, they didn't think you could read, porque eras mexicano [because you were Mexican]. They wouldn't give you good stuff and they would make us write crap like "What I Did on My Vacation," or "My Enemy," or "My Most Embarrassing Moment." We weren't allowed to read much.

In high school I got into American literature. I was really taken with the Graveyard Poets,[7] which is natural for

---

7. Graveyard Poets in the 1700s, English and Scottish poets who wrote about death

a fourteen-year-old; the age of reflection and all that. Steinbeck[8] I liked very much. The movie *The Grapes of Wrath* led me to read all his novels. I got into Hemingway;[9] read everything he had written. Walt Whitman[10] became a very important source, not only of inspiration, but at one point he seemed like the only connection that made sense, in almost a religious way. I dropped out of the Catholic Church at about fourteen—not dropped out, really, I just didn't want to have anything to do with religion right then. By the time of high school graduation I was reading about religion and I became pretty cynical. Well, Walt Whitman was my replacement: "I sing the body electric." Powerful things like that.

After that I got more and more into American and English literature. The Spanish came later. . . .

Has formal education helped or hindered you as a writer?

I think it has helped me in several ways. First of all, it allowed me to see better the context of what I write and of the literature emerging from the Chicano Movement within the whole idea of literature itself. Because of the training I have a more total picture. If a person has not had any, or has had very little training in literature, he or she could not see it in that context. I prefer to see Chicano literature within the context of all these other literatures. I can see it a lot better. Es decir, creo que hay mucho más

---

8. **Steinbeck** (STEYEN-bek) John Steinbeck, a well-known U.S. novelist and short-story writer who lived from 1902–1968
9. **Hemingway** (HEM-ihng-way) Ernest Hemingway, a well-known U.S. novelist and short-story writer who lived from 1899–1961
10. **Walt Whitman** (WAWLT WHIHT-muhn) a well-known U.S. poet who lived from 1819–92

ensimismamiento en aquellas personas que no tienen preparación [That is to say, I think that uneducated people are much more absorbed in themselves] and they think they're inventing everything under the sun. Now, maybe it's good; maybe they're more courageous that way.

Probably, I wanted to write because I had read, and the more you read, the more you want to write yourself. I think it does happen that way. . . .

AFTER YOU READ

Exchanging Backgrounds and Cultures

1. What important lesson does Rivera learn from his grandfather? How do his grandfather's values influence Rivera's future?

2. How does his father help Rivera with his reading? Why do you think he does this?

3. What does Rivera's use of both English and Spanish suggest about his attitude toward his cultural identity?

What Do You Think?

Of all the topics Rivera discusses in the interview, what is most meaningful to you?

Experiencing Nonfiction

An interview reveals much about the interviewee's values, interests, and beliefs. For instance, Rivera's interview shows readers the ways in which family, cultural history, and education shaped his career as a writer. Think about a person in your life whom you admire. Perhaps the person is a relative, friend, community leader, teacher, or classmate. Prepare a list of questions you would ask in order to discover more about that person's interests, values, and goals. After you have conducted the interview, write the questions and responses that best describe the person.

Optional Activity Conduct an imaginary interview with a famous personality, such as a well-known doctor, teacher, lawyer, or scientist. To make the interview more meaningful and accurate, first you might want to do research on the person's life. Then, present the information you have gathered in a series of questions and answers. Remember to ask questions, like those in the Rivera interview, that will reveal the experiences and events that influenced your subject's career.

UNIT 1: FOCUS ON WRITING

Nonfiction tells about real-life events, people, and places. There are many types of nonfiction, including essays, editorials, news stories, and autobiographies. For instance, in her autobiographical essay, Mary Helen Ponce describes a memorable childhood experience.

Writing Nonfiction

Choose one of the following two topics: Write an autobiographical account, or an essay, in which you describe an important personal experience; interview a friend or relative about his or her background.

The Writing Process

Good writing requires both time and effort. An effective writer completes a number of stages that together make up the writing process. The stages of the writing process are given below to help guide you through your assignment.

Prewriting

After you have decided what type of nonfiction you want to write, explore possible topics. One way to collect writing ideas is to interview a classmate. Ask each other questions relating to your experiences or to current events. Record your responses to your classmate's questions. Then, look over your responses for possible writing topics.

Once you have chosen your topic, consider whether it is narrow enough to be covered in the nonfiction form you selected. If not, divide it into subtopics. Then, review those subtopics and use one as the focus of your writing.

Next, consider your audience and purpose. For whom are you writing? Does your audience know about your topic or will you have to provide background information? Is your purpose to describe, to explain, or to persuade?

Once you have determined your audience and purpose, generate a list of specific details relating to your topic. For example, if you are writing about a personal experience, list the people, places, and events involved in that experience. Then, think of descriptive details connected with those people, places, and events.

Organize your details into an outline. Then, study your outline to see if you need to add more specific details. Eliminate those that are unimportant or unrelated to your purpose.

Drafting and Revising

After you have organized your ideas and details, begin your first draft. Keep your audience and purpose in mind as you write. Draw from your prewriting notes and outline. Feel free to include ideas and details that occur to you as you are writing.

When you have finished your first draft, put your composition aside for a day or two. In this way, you will have a fresh view when you begin revising. As you revise, make sure that you have included enough facts, reasons, and details to support your main idea. Also, make sure that you have presented your ideas in a clear, logical order. For example, David F. Gomez presents the events of his childhood in time order. Finally, consider whether the connections among the ideas and details in your writing are clear.

Proofreading and Publishing

After you have finished revising your final draft, carefully proofread your work. Correct any errors in spelling, grammar, punctuation, and capitalization. Then, make a neat final copy of your work.

Consider sharing your writing with your family or classmates. Perhaps you would like to submit it to your school newspaper or literary magazine.

FICTION OF THE MEXICAN AMERICANS

Works of fiction in any culture and in any language spring from the imaginations of writers. The pieces may be short or long, fantastic or realistic. Whatever the time, place, or plot, fiction offers a unique view of a situation. Each story reflects the personal experiences, knowledge, and concerns of the author.

The short story and the novel are two forms of modern fiction. A novel is longer than a short story, but both share certain story elements. The ways authors use these elements, however, vary greatly. The **setting** of a story is the time and place in which it occurs. The **characters** are the people in a story. The **plot** is the events that happen as a character or characters try to solve a problem or reach a goal. The **theme** is the author's message, or what the author wants a reader to understand about the subject. The **point of view** involves the narrator, or who is telling the story.

As you will discover, the stories in this section reflect a variety of settings and characters. They all explore the cultural heritages and experiences of their Mexican American authors and deal with themes important to Mexican American literature. These themes include the search for identity, the importance of family and home, the relationship between Mexican Americans and mainstream society, and the hardships of migrant workers. Despite their different themes and plots, the stories express powerful emotions and will leave you thinking about what you have read long after you have closed this book.

Sueño de Sonia. (Sonia's Dream.) Pastel by Sam Coronado. Co-founder of the Chicano Art Students Association at the University of Texas in Austin, Coronado teaches design at Austin Community College and has been active in promoting Hispanic art.

INTRODUCTION
My Wonder Horse

Born in Santa Fe, New Mexico, in 1919, Sabine Reyes Ulibarrí (sah-BEE-neh RAY-ez oo-lee-bahr-REE) grew up in Tierra Amarilla (tee-AYR-rah ahm-ah-REE-yah), a town high in the mountains of northern New Mexico. His years there impressed upon him a love for the culture and language of his ancestors. Both loves have influenced Ulibarrí's entire adult life. His long teaching and writing career has focused on preserving the values, beliefs, literature, and language in which he was raised.

Ulibarrí earned his Master's degree at the University of New Mexico and his doctorate in Spanish literature at UCLA. He returned to the University of New Mexico in 1959. At that time, he began the first of many years of teaching and writing about Spanish literature, as well as reciting Spanish poetry.

The short story you are about to read, "My Wonder Horse," combines both a boyhood memory and a tale deeply rooted in Mexican American folklore. The selection describes a boy's "rite of passage," or growth, into manhood. This passage, which involves tests of skill, strength, and courage, enables the boy to make discoveries about life and about himself.

My Wonder Horse

by Sabine Reyes Ulibarrí

He was white. White as memories lost. He was free. Free as happiness is. He was fantasy, liberty, and excitement. He filled and dominated the mountain valleys and surrounding plains. He was a white horse that flooded my youth with dreams and poetry.

Around the campfires of the country and in the sunny patios of the town, the ranch hands talked about him with enthusiasm and admiration. But gradually their eyes would become hazy and blurred with dreaming. The lively talk would die down. All thoughts fixed on the vision evoked by the horse. Myth of the animal kingdom. Poem of the world of men.

White and mysterious, he paraded his harem[1] through the summer forests with lordly rejoicing. Winter sent him to the plains and sheltered hillsides for the protection of his females. He spent the summer like an Oriental potentate[2] in his woodland gardens. The winter he passed like an illustrious warrior celebrating a well-earned victory.

He was a legend. The stories told of the Wonder Horse were endless. Some true, others fabricated. So many

---

1. **harem** (HAIR-uhm) *n.* a group of female animals
2. **potentate** (POHT-uhn-tayt) *n.* a ruler who has great power

traps, so many snares, so many searching parties, and all in vain. The horse always escaped, always mocked his pursuers, always rose above the control of man. Many a valiant cowboy swore to put his halter and his brand on the animal. But always he had to confess later that the mystic horse was more of a man than he.

I was fifteen years old. Although I had never seen the Wonder Horse, he filled my imagination and fired my ambition. I used to listen open-mouthed as my father and the ranch hands talked about the phantom horse who turned into mist and air and nothingness when he was trapped. I joined in the universal obsession—like the hope of winning the lottery—of putting my lasso on him some day, of capturing him and showing him off on Sunday afternoons when the girls of the town strolled through the streets.

It was high summer. The forests were fresh, green, and gay. The cattle moved slowly, fat and sleek in the August sun and shadow. Listless and drowsy in the lethargy of late afternoon, I was dozing on my horse. It was time to round up the herd and go back to the good bread of the cowboy camp. Already my comrades would be sitting around the campfire, playing the guitar, telling stories of past or present, or surrendering to the languor[3] of the late afternoon. The sun was setting behind me in a riot of streaks and colors. Deep, harmonious silence.

I sit drowsily still, forgetting the cattle in the glade. Suddenly the forest falls silent, a deafening quiet. The afternoon comes to a standstill. The breeze stops blowing, but it vibrates. The sun flares hotly. The planet, life, and time itself have stopped in an inexplicable way. For a moment, I don't understand what is happening.

Then my eyes focus. There he is! The Wonder Horse!

---

3. **languor** (LAN-guhr) *n.* feeling of being listless or sluggish

At the end of the glade, on high ground surrounded by summer green. He is a statue. He is an engraving. Line and form and white stain on a green background. Pride, prestige, and art incarnate[4] in animal flesh. A picture of burning beauty and virile freedom. An ideal, pure and invincible, rising from the eternal dreams of humanity. Even today my being thrills when I remember him.

A sharp neigh. A far-reaching challenge that soars on high, ripping the virginal fabric of the rosy clouds. Ears at the point. Eyes flashing. Tail waving active defiance. Hoofs glossy and destructive. Arrogant ruler of the countryside.

The moment is never ending, a momentary eternity. It no longer exists, but it will always live. . . . There must have been mares. I did not see them. The cattle went on their indifferent way. My horse followed them, and I came slowly back from the land of dreams to the world of toil. But life could no longer be what it was before.

That night under the stars I didn't sleep. I dreamed. How much I dreamed awake and how much I dreamed asleep, I do not know. I only know that a white horse occupied my dreams and filled them with vibrant sound, and light, and turmoil.

Summer passed and winter came. Green grass gave place to white snow. The herds descended from the mountains to the valleys and the hollows. And in the town they kept saying that the Wonder Horse was roaming through this or that secluded area. I inquired everywhere for his whereabouts. Every day he became for me more of an ideal, more of an idol, more of a mystery.

It was Sunday. The sun had barely risen above the snowy mountains. My breath was a white cloud. My horse was trembling with cold and fear like me. I left without

---

4. **incarnate** (ihn-KAHR-niht) *adj.* in a form that can be seen

44

going to mass. Without any breakfast. Without the usual bread and sardines in my saddle bags. I had slept badly, but had kept the vigil well. I was going in search of the white light that galloped through my dreams.

On leaving the town for the open country, the roads disappear. There are no tracks, human or animal. Only a silence, deep, white, and sparkling. My horse breaks trail with his chest and leaves an unending wake, an open rift, in the white sea. My trained, concentrated gaze covers the landscape from horizon to horizon, searching for the noble silhouette of the talismanic[5] horse.

It must have been midday. I don't know. Time had lost its meaning. I found him! On a slope stained with sunlight. We saw one another at the same time. Together, we turned to stone. Motionless, absorbed, and panting, I gazed at his beauty, his pride, his nobility. As still as sculptured marble, he allowed himself to be admired.

A sudden, violent scream breaks the silence. A glove hurled into my face. A challenge and a mandate. Then something surprising happens. The horse that in summer takes his stand between any threat and his herd, swinging back and forth from left to right, now plunges into the snow. Stronger than they, he is breaking trail for his mares. They follow him. His flight is slow in order to conserve his strength.

I follow. Slowly. Quivering. Thinking about his intelligence. Admiring his courage. Understanding his courtesy. The afternoon advances. My horse is taking it easy.

One by one the mares become weary. One by one, they drop out of the trail. Alone! He and I. My inner ferment bubbles to my lips. I speak to him. He listens and is quiet.

---

5. **talismanic** (tal-ihz-MAN-ihk) *adj.* bearing good luck

He still opens the way, and I follow in the path he leaves me. Behind us a long, deep trench crosses the white plain. My horse, which has eaten grain and good hay, is still strong. Undernourished as the Wonder Horse is, his strength is waning. But he keeps on because that is the way he is. He does not know how to surrender.

I now see black stains over his body. Sweat and the wet snow have revealed the black skin beneath the white hair. Snorting breath, turned to steam, tears the air. White spume above white snow. Sweat, spume, and steam. Uneasiness.

I felt like an executioner. But there was no turning back. The distance between us was growing relentlessly shorter. God and Nature watched indifferently.

I feel sure of myself at last. I untie the rope. I open the lasso and pull the reins tight. Every nerve, every muscle is tense. My heart is in my mouth. Spurs pressed against trembling flanks. The horse leaps. I whirl the rope and throw the obedient lasso.

A frenzy of fury and rage. Whirlpools of light and fans of transparent snow. A rope that whistles and burns the saddle tree. Smoking, fighting gloves. Eyes burning in their sockets. Mouth parched. Fevered forehead. The whole earth shakes and shudders. The long, white trench ends in a wide, white pool.

Deep, gasping quiet. The Wonder Horse is mine! Both still trembling, we look at one another squarely for a long time. Intelligent and realistic, he stops struggling and even takes a hesitant step toward me. I speak to him. As I talk, I approach him. At first, he flinches and recoils. Then he waits for me. The two horses greet one another in their own way. Finally, I succeed in stroking his mane. I tell him many things, and he seems to understand.

Ahead of me, along the trail already made, I drove him toward the town. Triumphant. Exultant. Childish laughter gathered in my throat. With my newfound manliness, I controlled it. I wanted to sing, but I fought down the desire. I wanted to shout, but I kept quiet. It was the ultimate in happiness. It was the pride of the male adolescent. I felt myself a conqueror.

Occasionally the Wonder Horse made a try for his liberty, snatching me abruptly from my thoughts. For a few moments, the struggle was renewed. Then we went on.

It was necessary to go through the town. There was no other way. The sun was setting. Icy streets and people on the porches. The Wonder Horse full of terror and panic for the first time. He ran and my well-shod horse stopped him. He slipped and fell on his side. I suffered for him. The indignity. The humiliation. Majesty degraded. I begged him not to struggle, to let himself be led. How it hurt me that other people should see him like that!

Finally we reached home.

"What shall I do with you, Mago?[6] If I put you into the stable or the corral, you are sure to hurt yourself. Besides, it would be an insult. You aren't a slave. You aren't a servant. You aren't even an animal."

I decided to turn him loose in the fenced pasture. There, little by little, Mago would become accustomed to my friendship and my company. No animal had ever escaped from that pasture.

My father saw me coming and waited for me without a word. A smile played over his face, and a spark danced in his eyes. He watched me take the rope from Mago, and the two of us thoughtfully observed him move away. My father clasped my hand a little more firmly than usual and said, "That was a man's job." That was all. Nothing more was needed. We understood one another very well. I was playing the role of a real man, but the childish laughter

---

6. **Mago** (MAH-goh) *n.* magician, wizard

and shouting that bubbled up inside me almost destroyed the impression I wanted to create.

That night I slept little, and when I slept, I did not know that I was asleep. For dreaming is the same when one really dreams, asleep or awake. I was up at dawn. I had to go to see my Wonder Horse. As soon as it was light, I went out into the cold to look for him.

The pasture was large. It contained a grove of trees and a small gully. The Wonder Horse was not visible anywhere, but I was not worried. I walked slowly, my head full of the events of yesterday and my plans for the future. Suddenly I realized that I had walked a long way. I quicken my steps. I look apprehensively around me. I begin to be afraid. Without knowing it, I begin to run. Faster and faster.

He is not there. The Wonder Horse has escaped. I search every corner where he could be hidden. I follow his tracks. I see that during the night he walked incessantly, sniffing, searching for a way out. He did not find one. He made one for himself.

I followed the track that led straight to the fence. And I saw that the trail did not stop but continued on the other side. It was a barbed-wire fence. There was white hair on the wire. There was blood on the barbs. There were red stains on the snow and little drops in the hoofprints on the other side of the fence.

I stopped there. I did not go any further. The rays of the morning sun on my face. Eyes clouded and yet filled with light. Childish tears on the cheeks of a man. A cry stifled in my throat. Slow silent sobs.

Standing there, I forgot myself and the world and time. I cannot explain it, but my sorrow was mixed with pleasure. I was weeping with happiness. No matter how much it hurt me, I was rejoicing over the flight and the freedom of the Wonder Horse, the dimensions of his indomitable spirit. Now he would always be fantasy, freedom, and excitement. The Wonder Horse was transcendent.[7] He had enriched my life forever.

My father found me there. He came close without a word and laid his arm across my shoulders. We stood looking at the white trench with its flecks of red that led into the rising sun.

---

7. transcendent (tran-SEN-duhnt) *adj.* extraordinary

AFTER YOU READ

Exchanging Backgrounds and Cultures

1. Describe the Wonder Horse. Are the narrator's feelings about the Wonder Horse similar to the feelings of others in his community? In what ways?

2. The introduction mentions that this is a "rite of passage" story, in which the narrator leaves a part of his childhood behind and learns about life and about himself. What examples of growth can you find in the story? Why do you think that the horse's escape in the end makes the narrator feel both happy and sad?

3. What does this story reveal about the culture in which Ulibarrí was raised and about his Hispanic heritage?

What Do You Think?

Which part of this story is most surprising to you? Why is it so surprising?

Experiencing Fiction

In his short story, Ulibarrí reflects on a memory from his childhood through a young narrator's tale of victory, loss, and triumph. It is a story of personal discovery and change. Think about an experience in your life or in the life of someone you know that brought a new understanding or a new perspective about life. Write a short story that uses a narrator to describe the experience and the understanding gained from it.

Optional Activity Is there a legend about a "wonder" animal that has been passed down in your family or community? If so, what do you think it represents? Write a short story that involves this wonder animal and the effect it has on the story's narrator.

INTRODUCTION

My Name, Laughter, Four Skinny Trees, A Smart Cookie

Sandra Cisneros (SAHN-drah sees-NEH-rohs) is the daughter of a Mexican father and a Mexican American mother. Born in Chicago in 1954, she was the only girl in a family of six boys. Although she was surrounded by many who loved her, her childhood was filled with turmoil, economic hardship, loneliness, and little privacy. The family moved back and forth between Chicago and Mexico. In both places, Cisneros felt dominated by men and excluded from her brothers' lives. As a result, Cisneros often escaped into a world of books, where she found excitement and friendship of another kind. Soon she began to weave tales and create conversations inside her head.

Cisneros is a writer of fiction, nonfiction, and poetry, in addition to being a teacher and lecturer. She has received many honors and awards for her short story collections and poetry. The selections that follow are from *The House on Mango Street,* published in 1983. The book is a collection of vignettes, or short accounts of events, people, and feelings, based on Cisneros's own experiences, as told through the narrative voice of a young girl, Esperanza (es-peh-RAHN-sah).

My Name
from *The House on*
Mango Street

by Sandra Cisneros

In English my name means hope. In Spanish it means too many letters. It means sadness, it means waiting. It is like the number nine. A muddy color. It is the Mexican records my father plays on Sunday mornings when he is shaving, songs like sobbing.

It was my great-grandmother's name and now it is mine. She was a horse woman too, born like me in the Chinese year of the horse—which is supposed to be bad luck if you're born female—but I think this is a Chinese lie because the Chinese, like the Mexicans, don't like their women strong.

My great-grandmother. I would've liked to have known her, a wild horse of a woman, so wild she wouldn't marry. Until my great-grandfather threw a sack over her head and carried her off. Just like that, as if she were a fancy chandelier. That's the way he did it.

And the story goes she never forgave him. She looked out the window her whole life, the way so many women sit their sadness on an elbow. I wonder if she made the best with what she got or was she sorry because she couldn't be all the things she wanted to be. Esperanza.[1] I have

---

1. **Esperanza** (ays-per-AHN-sah) *n.* a name

52

inherited her name, but I don't want to inherit her place by the window.

At school they say my name funny as if the syllables were made out of tin and hurt the roof of your mouth. But in Spanish my name is made out of a softer something, like silver, not quite as thick as sister's name—Magdalena[2]—which is uglier than mine. Magdalena who at least can come home and become Nenny. But I am always Esperanza.

I would like to baptize myself under a new name, a name more like the real me, the one nobody sees. Esperanza as Lisandra[3] or Maritza[4] or Zeze the X.[5] Yes. Something like Zeze the X will do.

---

2. **Magdalena** (mahg-dah-LAY-nah)
3. **Lisandra** (lee-SAHN-drah)
4. **Maritza** (mah-REET-sah)
5. **Zeze the X** (SAY-SAY thuh AY-kees)

Laughter
from *The House on Mango Street*

by Sandra Cisneros

Nenny and I don't look like sisters . . . not right away. Not the way you can tell with Rachel and Lucy who have the same fat popsicle lips like everybody else in their family. But me and Nenny, we are more alike than you would know. Our laughter for example. Not the shy ice cream bells giggle of Rachel and Lucy's family, but all of a sudden and surprised like a pile of dishes breaking. And other things I can't explain.

One day we were passing a house that looked, in my mind, like houses I had seen in Mexico. I don't know why. There was nothing about the house that looked exactly like the houses I remembered. I'm not even sure why I thought it, but it seemed to feel right.

Look at that house, I said, it looks like Mexico.

Rachel and Lucy look at me like I'm crazy, but before they can let out a laugh, Nenny says: Yes, that's Mexico all right. That's what I was thinking exactly.

Four Skinny Trees from *The House on Mango Street*

by Sandra Cisneros

They are the only ones who understand me. I am the only one who understands them. Four skinny trees with skinny necks and pointy elbows like mine. Four who do not belong here but are here. Four raggedy excuses planted by the city. From our room we can hear them, but Nenny just sleeps and doesn't appreciate these things.

Their strength is secret. They send ferocious roots beneath the ground. They grow up and they grow down and grab the earth between their hairy toes and bite the sky with violent teeth and never quit their anger. This is how they keep.

Let one forget his reason for being, they'd all droop like tulips in a glass, each with their arms around the other. Keep, keep, keep, trees say when I sleep. They teach.

When I am too sad and too skinny to keep keeping, when I am a tiny thing against so many bricks, then it is I look at trees. When there is nothing left to look at on this street. Four who grew despite concrete. Four who reach and do not forget to reach. Four whose only reason is to be and be.

A Smart Cookie from *The House on Mango Street*

by Sandra Cisneros

I could've been somebody, you know? my mother says and sighs. She has lived in this city her whole life. She can speak two languages. She can sing an opera. She knows how to fix a T.V. But she doesn't know which subway train to take to get downtown. I hold her hand very tight while we wait for the right train to arrive.

She used to draw when she had time. Now she draws with a needle and thread, little knotted rosebuds, tulips made of silk thread. Someday she would like to go to the ballet. Someday she would like to see a play. She borrows opera records from the public library and sings with velvety lungs powerful as morning glories.[1]

Today while cooking oatmeal she is Madame Butterfly[2] until she sighs and points the wooden spoon at me. I could've been somebody, you know? Esperanza, you go to school. Study hard. That Madame Butterfly was a fool. She stirs the oatmeal. Look at my *comadres*.[3] She

---

1. **morning glories** (MAWR-nihng GLAWR-eez) *n. pl.* trumpet-shaped flowers that grow on a vine and bloom in the morning
2. **Madame Butterfly** (MAD-uhm BUT-uhr-fleye) a tragic character in an opera by Puccini
3. **comadres** (kohm-AH-drays) *n. pl.* best friends

means Izaura[4] whose husband left and Yolanda[5] whose husband is dead. Got to take care all your own, she says shaking her head.

Then out of nowhere:

Shame is a bad thing, you know. It keeps you down. You want to know why I quit school? Because I didn't have nice clothes. No clothes, but I had brains.

Yup, she says disgusted, stirring again. I was a smart cookie then.

---

4. Izaura (ee-SOW-rah)
5. Yolanda (yoh-LAHN-duh)

AFTER YOU READ

Exchanging Backgrounds and Cultures

1. What does the narrator, Esperanza, reveal about herself, her family, and her Mexican American culture in these vignettes?

2. Why does Esperanza have conflicting feelings about her name? What does Mango Street represent for her?

3. How does remembering one's past and exploring it through fiction help a writer? In what ways can a writer's work benefit a reader?

What Do You Think?

Which of the vignettes included here from *The House on Mango Street* makes the strongest impression on you? Why is this selection meaningful?

Experiencing Fiction

In "My Name," the narrator explains for whom she was named, what her name means, and how she feels about it. Try to discover the origin and meaning of your name, and write about your search by creating a narrator to describe it. Were you named after a relative? Would you choose a new name if you could? What name would you choose, and why? Let your narrator explore these thoughts.

Optional Activity In what ways does Esperanza compare herself to the trees in "Four Skinny Trees"? What do these comparisons tell you about how she sees herself? To which animal or plant would you compare yourself? Explain your thinking.

INTRODUCTION
Growing Up

Gary Soto is a Chicano, or Mexican American, writer whose poetry, short story collections, and autobiographical essays have won many honors and awards. Born in 1952 in Fresno, California, Soto grew up in a world of Mexican American factory workers and field laborers. Soto's own life—as well as the lives of many other workers—was one of poverty. It left him feeling self-conscious and withdrawn.

Eager to escape the circumstances of his youth, Soto attended California State University and graduated with honors in 1974. Then, he studied creative writing at the University of California at Irvine. While he was still a student there, he had poems published in many magazines. These poems often reflect the hard work and pain of the factory workers and field laborers with whom Soto shared so much unhappiness as a youth.

Upon graduating from the University of California, he became a guest speaker at colleges and continued to write poetry. He also began to reflect upon his childhood experiences and the universal problems of growing up. Soto's autobiographical essays and many of his short stories focus on these themes. The short story "Growing Up" is just such a story.

Growing Up

by Gary Soto

Now that Maria was a tenth-grader, she felt she was too grown-up to have to go on family vacations. Last year, the family had driven three hundred miles to see their uncle in West Covina. There was nothing to do. The days were hot, with a yellow sky thick with smog they could feel on their fingertips. They played cards and watched game shows on television. After the first four days of doing nothing while the grown-ups sat around talking, the kids finally got to go to Disneyland.

Disneyland stood tall with castles and bright flags. The Matterhorn had wild dips and curves that took your breath away if you closed your eyes and screamed. The Pirates of the Caribbean didn't scare anyone but was fun anyway, and so were the teacups and It's a Small World. The parents spoiled the kids, giving each of them five dollars to spend on trinkets. Maria's younger sister, Irma, bought a Pinocchio coloring book and a candy bracelet. Her brothers, Rudy and John, spent their money on candy that made their teeth blue.

Maria saved her money. She knew everything was overpriced, like the Mickey Mouse balloons you could get for a fraction of the price in Fresno. Of course, the balloon at Hanoian's supermarket didn't have a Mickey Mouse face, but it would bounce and float and eventually pop like any other balloon.

Maria folded her five dollars, tucked it in her red purse, and went on rides until she got sick. After that, she sat on a bench, jealously watching other teenage girls who seemed much better dressed than she was. She felt stricken by poverty. All the screaming kids in nice clothes probably came from homes with swimming pools in their backyards, she thought. Yes, her father was a foreman[1] at a paper mill, and yes, she had a Dough-boy swimming pool in her backyard, but *still*, things were not the same. She had felt poor, and her sun dress, which seemed snappy in Fresno, was out of style at Disneyland, where every other kid was wearing Esprit shirts and Guess jeans.

This year Maria's family planned to visit an uncle in San Jose. Her father promised to take them to Great America, but she knew that the grown-ups would sit around talking for days before they remembered the kids and finally got up and did something. They would have to wait until the last day before they could go to Great America. It wasn't worth the boredom.

"Dad, I'm not going this year," Maria said to her father. He sat at the table with the newspaper in front of him.

"What do you mean?" he asked, slowly looking up. He thought a moment and said, "When I was a kid we didn't have the money for vacations. I would have been happy to go with my father."

"I know, I know. You've said that a hundred times," she snapped.

"What did you say?" he asked, pushing his newspaper aside.

Everything went quiet. Maria could hear the hum of the refrigerator and her brothers out in the front yard arguing over a popsicle stick, and her mother in the

---

1. **foreman** (FAWR-muhn) *n.* a man in charge of workers in a factory or mill

backyard watering the strip of grass that ran along the patio.

Her father's eyes locked on her with a dark stare. Maria had seen that stare before. She pleaded in a soft daughterly voice, "We never do anything. It's boring. Don't you understand?"

"No, I don't understand. I work all year, and if I want to go on a vacation, then I go. And my family goes too." He took a swallow of ice water, and glared.

"You have it so easy," he continued. "In Chihuahua,[2] my town, we worked hard. You worked, even *los chavalos!*[3] And you showed respect to your parents, something you haven't learned."

Here it comes, Maria thought, stories about his childhood in Mexico. She wanted to stuff her ears with wads of newspaper to keep from hearing him. She could recite his stories word-for-word. She couldn't wait until she was in college and away from them.

"Do you know my father worked in the mines? That he nearly lost his life? And today his lungs are bad." He pounded his chest with hard, dirt-creased knuckles.

Maria pushed back her hair and looked out the window at her brothers running around in the front yard. She couldn't stand it anymore. She got up and walked away, and when he yelled for her to come back, she ignored him. She locked herself in her bedroom and tried to read *Seventeen*, though she could hear her father complaining to her mother, who had come in when she had heard the yelling.

"*Habla con tu mocosa,*"[4] she heard him say.

She heard the refrigerator door open. He was

---

2. **Chihuahua** (chee-WAH-wah) *n.* a Mexican state that shares a border with Texas and New Mexico
3. *los chavalos* (lohs chah-VAH-lohs) *n. pl.* the kids
4. *habla con tu mocosa* (AH-blah kohn too moh-KOH-sah) talk to that snotty kid of yours

probably getting a beer, a "cold one," as he would say. She flipped through the pages of her magazine and stopped at a Levi's ad of a girl about her age walking between two happy-looking guys on a beach. She wished she were that girl, that she had another life. She turned the page and thought, I bet you he gets drunk and drives crazy tomorrow.

Maria's mother was putting away a pitcher of Kool-Aid the boys had left out. She looked at her husband, who was fumbling with a wadded-up napkin. His eyes were dark, and his thoughts were on Mexico, where a father was respected and his word, right or wrong, was final. "Rafael,[5] she's growing up; she's a teenager. She talks like that, but she still loves you."

"Sure, and that's how she shows her love, by talking back to her father." He rubbed the back of his neck and turned his head trying to make the stiffness go away. He knew it was true, but he was the man of the house and no daughter of his was going to tell him what to do.

Instead, it was his wife, Eva, who told him what to do. "Let the girl stay. She's big now. She don't want to go on rides no more. She can stay with her *niña*."[6]

The father drank his beer and argued, but eventually agreed to let his daughter stay.

The family rose just after six the next day and was ready to go by seven-thirty. Maria stayed in her room. She wanted to apologize to her father but couldn't. She knew that if she said, "Dad, I'm sorry," she would break into tears. Her father wanted to come into her room and say, "We'll do something really special this vacation. Come with us, honey." But it was hard for him to show his emotions around his children, especially when he tried to make up to them.

---

5. **Rafael** (rahf-eye-AYL)
6. *niña* (NEEN-yah) *n.* Maria's godmother (from *madrina*, god-mother)

The mother kissed Maria. "Maria, I want you to clean the house and then walk over to your *niña*'s. I want no monkey business while we're gone, do you hear me?"

"*Sí*, Mama."

"Here's the key. You water the plants inside and turn on the sprinkler every couple of days." She handed Maria the key and hugged her. "You be good. Now, come say goodbye to your father."

Reluctantly, she walked out in her robe to the front yard and, looking down at the ground, said goodbye to her father. The father looked down and said goodbye to the garden hose at his feet.

After they left, Maria lounged in her pajamas listening to the radio and thumbing through magazines. Then she got up, fixed herself a bowl of Cocoa Puffs, and watched "American Bandstand." Her dream was to dance on the show, to look at the camera, smile, and let everyone in Fresno see that she could have a good time, too.

But an ill feeling stirred inside her. She felt awful about arguing with her father. She felt bad for her mother and two brothers, who would have to spend the next three hours in the car with him. Maybe he would do something crazy, like crash the car on purpose to get back at her, or fall asleep and run the car into an irrigation ditch. And it would be her fault.

She turned the radio to a news station. She listened for half an hour, but most of the news was about warships in the Persian Gulf and a tornado in Texas. There was no mention of her family.

Maria began to calm down because, after all, her father was really nice beneath his gruffness. She dressed slowly, made some swishes with the broom in the kitchen, and let the hose run in a flower bed while she painted her toenails with her mother's polish. Afterward, she called her friend Becky to tell her that her parents had let her stay home, that she was free—for five days at least.

"Great," Becky said. "I wish my mom and dad would

go away and let me stay by myself."

"No, I have to stay with my godmother." She made a mental note to give her *niña* a call. "Becky, let's go to the mall and check out the boys."

"All right."

"I'll be over pretty soon."

Maria called her *niña*, who said it was OK for her to go shopping, but to be at her house for dinnertime by six. After hanging up, Maria took off her jeans and T-shirt, and changed into a dress. She went through her mother's closet to borrow a pair of shoes and drenched her wrists in Charlie perfume. She put on coral-pink lipstick and a smudge of blue eyeshadow. She felt beautiful, although a little self-conscious. She took off some of the lipstick and ran water over her wrists to dilute the fragrance.

While she walked the four blocks to Becky's house, she beamed with happiness until she passed a man who was on his knees pulling weeds from his flower bed. At his side, a radio was reporting a traffic accident. A big rig had overturned after hitting a car near Salinas, twenty miles from San Jose.

A wave of fear ran through her. Maybe it was *them.* Her smile disappeared, and her shoulders slouched. No, it couldn't be, she thought. Salinas is not that close to San Jose. Then again, maybe her father wanted to travel through Salinas because it was a pretty valley with wide plains and oak trees, and horses and cows that stared as you passed them in your speeding car. But maybe it did happen; maybe they had gotten in an awful wreck.

By the time she got to Becky's house, she was riddled with guilt, since it was she who would have disturbed her father and made him crash.

"Hi," she said to Becky, trying to look cheerful.

"You look terrific, Maria," Becky said. "Mom, look at Maria. Come inside for a bit."

Maria blushed when Becky's mother said she looked gorgeous. She didn't know what to do except stare at the carpet and say, "Thank you, Mrs. Ledesma."

Becky's mother gave them a ride to the mall, but they'd have to take a bus back. The girls first went to Macy's, where they hunted for a sweater, something flashy but not too flashy. Then they left to have a Coke and sit by the fountain under an artificial tree. They watched people walk by, especially the boys, who, they agreed, were dumb but cute nevertheless.

They went to The Gap, where they tried on some skirts, and ventured into The Limited, where they walked up and down the aisles breathing in the rich smells of 100-percent wool and silk. They were about to leave, when Maria heard once again on someone's portable radio that a family had been killed in an auto accident near Salinas. Maria stopped smiling for a moment as she pictured her family's overturned Malibu station wagon.

Becky sensed that something was wrong and asked, "How come you're so quiet?"

Maria forced a smile. "Oh, nothing, I was just thinking."

" 'bout what?"

Maria thought quickly. "Oh, I think I left the water on at home." This could have been true. Maria remembered pulling the hose from the flower bed, but couldn't remember if she had turned the water off.

Afterward they rode the bus home with nothing to show for their three hours of shopping except a small bag of See's candies. But it had been a good day. Two boys had followed them, joking and flirting, and they had flirted back. The girls gave them made-up telephone numbers, then turned away and laughed into their hands.

"They're fools," Becky said, "but cute."

Maria left Becky when they got off the bus, and started

off to her *niña*'s house. Then she remembered that the garden hose might still be running at home. She hurried home, clip-clopping clumsily in her mother's shoes.

The garden hose was rolled neatly against the trellis. Maria decided to check the mail and went inside. When she pushed open the door, the living room gave off a quietness she had never heard before. Usually the TV was on, her younger brothers and sister were playing, and her mother could be heard in the kitchen. When the telephone rang, Maria jumped. She kicked off her shoes, ran to the phone, and picked up the receiver only to hear a distant clicking sound.

"Hello, hello?" Maria's heart began to thump. Her mind went wild with possibilities. An accident, she thought, they're in an accident, and it's all my fault. "Who is it? Dad? Mom?"

She hung up and looked around the room. The clock on the television set glowed 5:15. She gathered the mail, changed into jeans, and left for her *niña*'s house with a shopping bag containing her nightie and a toothbrush.

Her *niña* was happy to see her. She took Maria's head in her hands and gave it a loud kiss.

"Dinner is almost ready," she said, gently pulling her inside.

"Oh, good. Becky and I only had popcorn for lunch."

They had a quiet evening together. After dinner, they sat on the porch watching the stars. Maria wanted to ask her *niña* if she had heard from her parents. She wanted to know if the police had called to report that they had gotten into an accident. But she just sat on the porch swing, letting anxiety eat a hole in her soul.

The family was gone for four days. Maria prayed for them, prayed that she would not wake up to a phone call saying that their car had been found in a ditch. She made a list of the ways she could be nicer to them: doing the dishes without being asked, watering the lawn, hugging her father after work, and playing with her youngest brother, even if it bored her to tears.

At night Maria worried herself sick listening to the radio for news of an accident. She thought of her uncle Shorty and how he fell asleep and crashed his car in the small town of Mendota. He lived confined to a motorized wheelchair and was scarred with burns on the left side of his face.

"Oh, please, don't let anything like that happen to them," she prayed.

In the morning she could barely look at the newspaper. She feared that if she unfolded it, the front page would feature a story about a family from Fresno who had flown off the roller coaster at Great America. Or that a shark had attacked them as they bobbed happily among the white-tipped waves. Something awful is going to happen, she said to herself as she poured Rice Krispies into a bowl.

But nothing happened. Her family returned home, dark from lying on the beach and full of great stories about the Santa Cruz boardwalk and Great America and an Egyptian museum. They had done more this year than in all their previous vacations.

"Oh, we had fun," her mother said, pounding sand from her shoes before entering the house.

Her father gave her a tight hug as her brothers ran by, dark from hours of swimming.

Maria stared at the floor, miffed. How dare they have so much fun? While she worried herself sick about them, they had splashed in the waves, stayed at Great America until nightfall, and eaten at all kinds of restaurants. They even went shopping for fall school clothes.

Feeling resentful as Johnny described a ride that dropped straight down and threw your stomach into your mouth, Maria turned away and went off to her bedroom, where she kicked off her shoes and thumbed through an old *Seventeen.* Her family was alive and as obnoxious as ever. She took back all her promises. From now on she would keep to herself and ignore them. When they asked, "Maria, would you help me," she would pretend not to hear and walk away.

"They're heartless," she muttered. "Here I am worrying about them, and there they are having fun." She thought of the rides they had gone on, the hours of body surfing, the handsome boys she didn't get to see, the restaurants, and the museum. Her eyes filled with tears. For the first time in years, she hugged a doll, the one her grandmother Lupe had stitched together from rags and old clothes.

"Something's wrong with me," she cried softly. She turned on her radio and heard about a single-engined plane that had crashed in Cupertino, a city not far from San Jose. She thought of the plane and the people inside, how the pilot's family would suffer:

She hugged her doll. Something was happening to her, and it might be that she was growing up. When the news ended, and a song started playing, she got up and washed her face without looking in the mirror.

That night the family went out for Chinese food. Although her brothers fooled around, cracked jokes, and spilled a soda, she was happy. She ate a lot, and when her fortune cookie said, "You are mature and sensible," she had to agree. And her father and mother did too. The family drove home singing the words to "La Bamba" along with the car radio.

AFTER YOU READ

Exchanging Backgrounds and Cultures

1. What is the setting of the story? How do you know? Why do you think the author chose this setting?

2. Describe the character of Maria. Why doesn't she want to go with her family on vacation? Why does she worry about them when they are gone?

3. Does this story reflect only the experiences of a Mexican American teenager, or could this happen to a teenager of any background? Explain your thoughts.

What Do You Think?

Which part of the story is especially meaningful to you? Why is it important?

Experiencing Fiction

Gary Soto explores his own experiences growing up through the fictional character of Maria. Write a short story that draws upon an experience in your life by creating a fictional character who goes through that experience. Use a setting you know and be sure to include descriptions and dialogue that help readers understand who your characters are and how they feel.

Optional Activity Interesting stories are often inspired by the events of everyday life. Think about your school experiences. Has something happened in school that made a strong impression on you? Write a short story based on that event. Create fictional characters, descriptions, and dialogue to describe what you experienced.

INTRODUCTION
And the Earth Did Not Devour Him

Tomás Rivera was a much-respected poet, prose writer, scholar, and educator. He left a wealth of short stories, poems, essays, and one novel. He also left a lasting mark on the universities with which he was associated.

Rivera was born in 1935 in Crystal City, Texas, to parents who were migrant workers. His childhood was a mixture of laboring in the fields when necessary, attending school when possible, and reading books and magazines whenever he could find them. His adult life was quite different. In addition to his writing career, he earned several degrees and served as chancellor of the University of California at Riverside. He remained chancellor until his death in 1984.

Much of Rivera's writing focuses on the people and experiences of his youth—the Mexican American migrant workers of the 1940s and 1950s who coped with poverty and mistreatment, and were constantly moving in search of work. His award-winning novel, . . . y no se lo tragó la tierra, explores these experiences through a series of stories or episodes. The stories describe a year in the life of an unnamed migrant boy through his thoughts, impressions, and memories. The excerpt you will read reveals some of these memories.

And the Earth Did Not Devour Him

by Tomás Rivera

The first time he felt hate and anger was when he saw his mother crying for his uncle and aunt. They both had caught tuberculosis[1] and had been sent to different sanitariums. So, between the brothers and sisters, they had distributed the children among themselves and had taken care of them as best they could. Then the aunt died, and soon thereafter they brought the uncle back from the sanitarium, but he was already spitting blood. That was when he saw his mother crying every little while. He became angry because he was unable to do anything against anyone. Today he felt the same. Only today it was for his father.

"You all should've come home right away, m'ijo.[2] Couldn't you see that your Daddy was sick? You should have known that he was sunstruck. Why didn't you come home?"

"I don't know. Us being so soaked with sweat, we didn't feel so hot, but I guess that when you're sunstruck it's different. But I did tell him to sit down under the tree

---

1. **tuberculosis** (tuh-ber-kyuh-LOH-sihs) *n.* a contagious lung disease
2. **m'ijo** (MEE-hoh) *n.* my son

that's at the edge of the rows, but he didn't want to. And that was when he started throwing up. Then we saw he couldn't hoe anymore and we dragged him and put him under a tree. He didn't even say a word."

"Poor viejo, my poor viejo.[3] Last night he hardly slept. Didn't you hear him outside the house. He squirmed in bed all night with cramps. God willing, he'll get well. I've been giving him cool lemonade all day, but his eyes still look glassy. If I'd gone to the fields yesterday, I tell you he wouldn't have gotten sick. My poor viejo, he's going to have cramps all over his body for three days and three nights at the least. Now, you all take care of yourselves. Don't overwork yourselves so much. Don't pay any mind to that boss if he tries to rush you. Just don't do it. He thinks it's so easy since he's not the one who's out there, stooped."

He became even angrier when he heard his father moan outside the chicken coop. He wouldn't stay inside because he said it made him feel very nervous. Outside where he could feel the fresh air was where he got some relief. And also when the cramps came he could roll over on the grass. Then he thought about whether his father might die from the sunstroke. At times he heard his father start to pray and ask for God's help. At first he had faith that he would get well soon but by the next day he felt the anger growing inside of him. And all the more when he heard his mother and his father clamoring for God's mercy. That night, well past midnight, he had been awakened by his father's groans. His mother got up and removed the scapularies[4] from around his neck and washed them. Then she lit some candles. But nothing happened. It was like his aunt and uncle all over again.

---

3. **viejo** (vee-AY-hoh) *n.* old man
4. **scapularies** (SKAP-yoo-luh-reez) *n. pl.* bandages

"What's to be gained from doing all that, Mother? Don't tell me you think it helped my aunt and uncle any. How come we're like this, like we're buried alive? Either the germs eat us alive or the sun burns us up. Always some kind of sickness. And every day we work and work. For what? Poor Dad, always working so hard. I think he was born working. Like he says, barely five years old and already helping his father plant corn. All the time feeding the earth and the sun, only to one day, just like that, get knocked down by the sun. And there you are, helpless. And them, begging for God's help . . . why, God doesn't care about us . . . I don't think there even is . . . No, better not say it, what if Dad gets worse. Poor Dad, I guess that at least gives him some hope.

His mother noticed how furious he was, and that morning she told him to calm down, that everything was in God's hands and that with God's help his father was going to get well.

"Oh, Mother, do you really believe that? I am certain that God has no concern for us. Now you tell me, is Dad evil or mean-hearted? You tell me if he has ever done any harm to anyone."

"Of course not."

"So there you have it. You see? And my aunt and uncle? You explain. And the poor kids, now orphans, never having known their parents. Why did God have to take them away? I tell you, God could care less about the poor. Tell me, why must we live here like this? What have we done to deserve this? You're so good and yet you have to suffer so much."

"Oh, please, m'ijo, don't talk that way. Don't speak against the will of God. Don't talk that way, please, m'ijo. You scare me. . . .

"Well, maybe. That way at least I could get rid of this anger. I'm so tired of thinking about it. Why? Why you?

Why Dad? Why my uncle? Why my aunt? Why their kids? Tell me, Mother, why? Why us, buried in the earth like animals with no hope for anything? You know the only hope we have is coming out here every year. And like you yourself say, only death brings rest. I think that's the way my aunt and uncle felt and that's how Dad must feel too."

"That's how it is, m'ijo. Only death brings us rest."

"But why us?"

"Well, they say that . . . "

"Don't say it. I know what you're going to tell me—that the poor go to heaven."

That day started out cloudy and he could feel the morning coolness brushing his eyelashes as he and his brothers and sisters began the day's labor. Their mother had to stay home to care for her husband. Thus, he felt responsible for hurrying on his brothers and sisters. During the morning, at least for the first few hours, they endured the heat but by ten-thirty the sun had suddenly cleared the skies and pressed down against the world. They began working more slowly because of the weakness, dizziness and suffocation they felt when they worked too fast. Then they had to wipe the sweat from their eyes every little while because their vision would get blurred.

"If you start blacking out, stop working, you hear me? Or go a little slower. When we reach the edge we'll rest a bit to get our strength back. It's gonna be hot today. If only it'd stay just a bit cloudy like this morning, then nobody would complain. But no, once the sun bears down like this not even one little cloud dares to appear out of fear. And the worst of it is we'll finish up here by two and then we have to go over to that other field that's nothing but hills. It's okay at the top of the hill but down in the lower part of the slopes it gets to be real suffocating. There's no breeze there. Hardly any air goes through. Remember?"

"Yeah."

"That's where the hottest part of the day will catch us.

Just drink plenty of water every little while. It don't matter if the boss gets mad. Just don't get sick. And if you can't go on, tell me right away, all right? We'll go home. Y'all saw what happened to Dad when he pushed himself too hard. The sun has no mercy, it can eat you alive."

Just as they had anticipated, they had moved on to the other field by early afternoon. By three o'clock they were all soaking with sweat. Not one part of their clothing was dry. Every little while they would stop. At times they could barely breathe, then they would black out and they would become fearful of getting sunstruck, but they kept on working.

"How do y'all feel?"

"Man, it's so hot! But we've got to keep on. 'Til six, at least. Except this water doesn't cut our thirst any. Sure wish I had a bottle of cool water, real cool, fresh from the well, or a coke, ice-cold."

"Are you crazy? That'd sure make you sunsick right now. Just don't work so fast. Let's see if we can make it until six. What do you think?"

At four o'clock the youngest became ill. He was only nine years old, but since he was paid the same as a grown up he tried to keep up with the rest. He began vomiting. He sat down, then he laid down. Terrified, the other children ran to where he lay and looked at him. It appeared that he had fainted and when they opened his eyelids they saw his eyes were rolled back. The next youngest child started crying but right away he told him to stop and help him carry his brother home. It seemed he was having cramps all over his little body. He lifted him and carried him by himself, and he began asking himself again, *why*?

"Why Dad and then my little brother? He's only nine years old. Why? He has to work like a mule buried in the earth. Dad, Mom, and my little brother here, what are they guilty of?"

Each step that he took towards the house resounded

with the question, *why?* About halfway to the house he began to get furious. Then he started crying out of rage. His little brothers and sisters did not know what to do, and they, too, started crying, but out of fear. Then he started cursing. And without even realizing it, he said what he had been wanting to say for a long time. He cursed God. Upon doing this he felt that fear instilled in him by the years and by his parents. For a second he saw the earth opening up to devour him. Then he felt his footsteps against the earth, compact, more solid than ever. Then his anger swelled up again, and he vented it by cursing God. He looked at his brother, he no longer appeared so sick. He didn't know whether his brothers and sisters had understood the enormity of his curse.

That night he did not fall asleep until very late. He felt at peace as never before. He felt as though he had become detached from everything. He no longer worried about his father nor his brother. All that he awaited was the new day, the freshness of the morning. By daybreak his father was doing better. He was on his way to recovery. And his little brother, too; the cramps had almost completely subsided. Frequently he felt a sense of surprise upon recalling what he had done the previous afternoon. He thought of telling his mother, but he decided to keep it a secret. All he told her was that the earth did not devour anyone, nor did the sun.

He left for work and encountered a very cool morning. There were clouds in the sky and for the first time he felt capable of doing and undoing anything that he pleased. He looked down at the earth and kicked it hard and said.

"Not yet, you can't swallow me up yet. Someday, yes. But I'll never know it.". . .

AFTER YOU READ

Exchanging Backgrounds and Cultures

1. How do the boy's feelings about his situation differ from those of his parents? Why does he feel such hate and rage?

2. What effect does nighttime have on the boy?

3. What does this episode reveal about the spirit of the Mexican American migrant worker?

What Do You Think?

Which part of this episode makes the greatest impact on you? Why is it so powerful?

Experiencing Fiction

When writers choose to tell a story from a particular character's perspective, they often have that character narrate from a first-person point of view. The character uses the word *I* instead of *he* or *she*. Rivera, however, uses the third-person point of view. In this novel, the boy uses *he* instead of *I* when he talks about himself. Why do you think he does this?

Think about the past year of your life. What thoughts and impressions come to mind? Is there an event that stands out? Write a fictional episode to capture that experience. Try using a third-person point of view as Rivera does. Be sure to include dialogue.

Optional Activity At the end of the episode, the boy expresses great spirit and determination, despite his suffering. Think about a person you know who has shown this strength in facing a problem. Write a fictional episode based on this person and his or her experience. Try using the third-person narrative as Rivera does in this excerpt.

UNIT 2: FOCUS ON WRITING

Unlike nonfiction, which is about real-life events, places, and people, fiction springs from a writer's imagination. However, writers of short stories and novels often draw upon their cultural backgrounds, their experiences, and their meetings with people they know. The authors in this unit use all these elements in their writing. For example, "My Wonder Horse" reflects both the storytelling tradition of Ulibarrí's heritage and his own childhood experiences in his hometown of Tierra Amarilla.

Writing a Short Story

Short stories capture characters caught up in a single conflict, or focus on one particular theme. Write a short story about an experience in your life or something you have learned from your heritage.

The Writing Process

Good writing requires both time and effort. An effective writer completes a number of stages that together make up the writing process. The stages of the writing process are given below to help guide you through your assignment.

Prewriting

Think about your past. Which memories stand out most clearly? List some of your ideas, then decide which one you might want to explore further. After selecting an idea, set up a chart with columns for each of the story elements: *setting, characters, conflict, plot,* and *theme.* Make notes in each column to help you shape your story. You might ask yourself the following questions:

Setting: When and where does the story take place? What words will I use to describe the sights and sounds of the place?

Characters: Who will be the main character? Which other characters will take part in the action?

Conflict: What is the central problem? Is it internal (within the character's mind) or external (between the character and some outside force)? In "My Wonder Horse," the conflict is both external and internal. The boy first struggles to capture the horse and then must understand his actions when he recognizes the horse's true nature.

Plot: What events will take place? What will be the high point, or climax, of the story? How will the conflict be resolved?

Theme: Will the story have a message? How will the story reveal this message or theme?

Before you begin to write, decide who the narrator of the story will be. A narrator can be a character in the story or someone who seems to be watching the events of the story as they happen. In *The House on Mango Street*, Sandra Cisneros uses one of her characters, Esperanza, as her narrator.

Drafting and Revising

Use your prewriting chart to write a draft of your story. Remember that the first draft is not the final version of the story. Include descriptions of sights and sounds and use dialogue.

When revising your short story, make sure that the descriptions and dialogue are important to the plot. Eliminate any passages that do not add to the action or the purpose of the story. If you have not already done so, now is the time to choose a title. The title should tell something about the story and also attract the reader's attention.

Proofreading and Publishing

Proofread your short story and correct any errors in spelling, grammar, punctuation, and capitalization. Then make a neat final copy.

You can share your story in several ways. Read it aloud to classmates, family, and friends, or submit it to a school literary magazine. You might want to add illustrations or photographs if your story is published in magazine form.

UNIT 3

POETRY OF THE MEXICAN AMERICANS

Poets use a variety of literary techniques to communicate meaning with just a few words. **Repetition,** the repeated use of any element of language, helps produce rhythm. Alliteration and parallelism are two important types of repetition. **Alliteration** is the repetition of consonant sounds at the beginnings of words or accented syllables. In the sentence "My fingers foolish before paper and pen/hide in my palms," from "Señora X No More," Pat Mora repeats the sounds of the letters *f* and *p* to create a bumpy effect. This illustrates how the character feels about her efforts to learn English. **Parallelism** is the repetition of words or phrases. In his poem "Old Man," Ricardo Sánchez creates a pattern by beginning each stanza with the same phrase. Parallelism helps link the various parts of a poem.

Figurative language uses figures of speech. A figure of speech is a way of saying one thing to add meaning to another. Two commonly used figures of speech are simile and metaphor. A **simile** compares two different objects using the words *like* or *as*. A **metaphor** is a comparison in which one thing is spoken of as though it were something else.

Imagery refers to a poet's use of words to create mental pictures. An image may appeal to any one of the five senses. In "My Father Is a Simple Man," Luis Omar Salinas portrays the hardships of life as a "punishing evil stranger."

In the first group of poems, the writers discover connections between their identities and their cultural roots. In the second group, the poets point to people and places that represent their Mexican American heritage. As you read, pay careful attention to the way in which literary techniques enhance the meaning of each poem.

Cuatro Parejas Folkloricas. (Four Couples Folk Dancing.)
Pastel by Tony Ortega. Ortega's work has been exhibited in
Colorado, New Mexico, Spain, and Mexico.

INTRODUCTION
Section 1: Self-Discovery

Through vivid imagery and figurative language, the poets presented in this section express their identities and their cultural heritages. By exploring family relationships and certain Mexican and U.S. customs and beliefs, these poets reveal that their sense of identity is rooted firmly in family and culture.

Luis Omar Salinas, a Mexican American poet born in Texas but raised in California, examines his relationship with his father in the poem "My Father Is a Simple Man." He recognizes the wisdom and courage in his father's simple and honest approach to the hardships of life. Much of Salinas's poetry deals with the loss of identity that many Mexican Americans experience after moving to the United States.

Alberto Ríos, a Mexican American poet from Nogales, Arizona, rejected his Mexican heritage as a child. But he rediscovered his language and culture in high school and in college. In the poem "Nani," Ríos examines a boy's relationship with his grandmother as a way of understanding his Mexican roots. In "Señora X No More" and "Picturesque: San Cristóbal de las Casas," Pat Mora captures the differences between the traditional ways of her Mexican ancestors and modern U.S. culture. Born and raised in El Paso, Texas, Mora has experienced firsthand changes in Mexican American culture as a result of daily contact with mainstream U.S. society.

My Father Is a Simple Man

by Luis Omar Salinas

I walk to town with my father
to buy a newspaper. He walks slower
than I do so I must slow up.
The street is filled with children.
We argue about the price
of pomegranates, I convince
him it is the fruit of scholars.
He has taken me on this journey
and it's been lifelong.
He's sure I'll be healthy
so long as I eat more oranges,
and tells me the orange
has seeds and so is perpetual;
and we too will come back
like the orange trees.
I ask him what he thinks
about death and he says
he will gladly face it when
it comes but won't jump
out in front of a car.
I'd gladly give my life
for this man with a sixth
grade education, whose kindness
and patience are true . . .

The truth of it is, he's the scholar,
and when the bitter-hard reality
comes at me like a punishing
evil stranger, I can always
remember that here was a man
who was a worker and provider,
who learned the simple facts
in life and lived by them,
who held no pretense.
And when he leaves without
benefit of fanfare or applause
I shall have learned what little
there is about greatness.

Nani[1]

by Alberto Ríos

Sitting at her table, she serves
the sopa de arroz[2] to me
instinctively, and I watch her,
the absolute *mamá*, and eat words
I might have had to say more
out of embarrassment. To speak,
now-foreign words I used to speak,
too, dribble down her mouth as she serves
me albóndigas.[3] No more

1. **Nani** (NAH-nee) *n.* nickname for his grandmother
2. **sopa de arroz** (SOH-pah day ah-ROHS) rice soup
3. **albóndigas** (ahl-BOHN-dee-gahs) *n. pl.* spicy meatballs

than a third are easy to me.
By the stove she does something with words
and looks at me only with her
back. I am full. I tell her
I taste the mint, and watch her speak
smiles at the stove. All my words
make her smile. Nani never serves
herself, she only watches me
with her skin, her hair. I ask for more.

I watch the *mamá* warming more
tortillas for me. I watch her
fingers in the flame for me.

Near her mouth, I see a wrinkle speak
of a man whose body serves
the ants like she serves me, then more words
about this and that, flowing more
easily from these other mouths. Each serves
as a tremendous string around her,
holding her together. They speak
Nani was this and that to me
and I wonder just how much of me
will die with her, what were the words
I could have been, was. Her insides speak
through a hundred wrinkles, now, more
than she can bear, steel around her,
shouting, then, What is this thing she serves?

She asks me if I want more.
I own no words to stop her.
Even before I speak, she serves.

Señora X No More

by Pat Mora

Straight as a nun I sit.
My fingers foolish before paper and pen
hide in my palms. I hear the slow, accented echo
          How are yu? I ahm fine. How are yu?
of the other women who clutch notebooks
and blush at their stiff lips resisting
sounds that float gracefully as
bubbles from their children's mouths.
My teacher bends over me, gently squeezes
my shoulders, the squeeze I give my sons,
hands louder than words.
She slides her arms around me:
a warm shawl, lifts my left arm
onto the cold, lined paper.
"*Señora,* don't let it slip away," she says
and opens the ugly, soap-wrinkled fingers
of my right hand with a pen like I pry open
the lips of a stubborn grandchild.
My hand cramps around the thin hardness.
"Let it breathe," says this woman who knows
my hand and tongue knot, but she guides
and I dig the tip of my pen into that white.
I carve my crooked name, and again at night
until my hand and arm are sore,
I carve my crooked name,
my name.

Picturesque: San Cristóbal de las Casas [1]

by Pat Mora

No one told me about the bare feet.

The Indians, yes
the turquoise and pink shawls, yes
the men running lightly on thin sidewalks
hats streaming with ribbons, yes
the chatter of women sunning outside the church
weaving bracelets with quick fingers, yes

but no one told me about the bare feet.

The smiles, yes
the babies slung on women's backs,
the bundles of huge white lilies
carried to market: fresh headdresses,
the young girls like morning birds gathering
for a feeding, pressing dolls into my hands, yes

but no one told me about the bare feet.

The weavers, yes
the hands that read threads,
the golden strings pulled from bushes
in fresh handfuls to steal a yellow dye,
the houses in the clouds, in the high hills,
shuttles to-and-fro, to-and
-fro on tight looms,[2] yes

---

1. **San Cristóbal de las Casas** (sahn krees-TOH-bahl day lahs KAH-sahs) Spanish for *Saint Christopher of the Houses,* a town in the state of Chiapas, in southern Mexico
2. **looms** (LOOMZ) *n. pl.* machines for weaving thread or yarn into cloth

but no one told me about the bare feet.
No one told me about the weaver's chair, a rock.
No one told me about the wood bundles bending
women's backs. No one told me about the children

who know to open their smiles
as they open their dry palms.

AFTER YOU READ

Exchanging Backgrounds and Cultures

1. In Salinas's poem "My Father Is a Simple Man," what does the speaker recognize about his father's attitude toward life? How does this quality influence the speaker's own attitude?

2. In "Nani" and "Señora X No More," what role does spoken or written language play in the identities of the two speakers?

3. In "Picturesque: San Cristóbal de las Casas," the speaker of the poem observes the people of San Cristóbal de las Casas, Mexico. How do the images in the poem show the speaker's feelings about what she sees?

What Do You Think?

Which poem in this group is especially meaningful to you? How does the use of imagery and language add to that effect?

Experiencing Poetry

The poets in this group make discoveries about themselves. Think about an experience in your own life that helped you learn about yourself. Then, write a short poem that reveals the connection between this experience and your own self-discovery.

Optional Activity Write a poem that conveys your impressions of a place you have visited. For instance, in Pat Mora's "Picturesque: San Cristóbal de las Casas," the speaker is surprised at the simple life in San Cristóbal de las Casas. Like Mora, who repeats the image of bare feet, use repetition to describe how the place makes you feel.

INTRODUCTION
Section 2:
Thinking About the Past

The three poets in this group look to the past to make better sense of the present. In their poems, they remember the people and places that represent their cultural roots. In Pat Mora's poem "Bailando," the speaker recalls how happy her aunt was as she danced on her 90th birthday. Like much of Mora's writing, the poem "Bailando" shows her love for the language, values, and customs of Mexican culture.

The next poem, "Old Man," was written by Ricardo Sánchez. Born in El Paso, Texas, in 1941, Sánchez often uses his writing to make people aware of the discrimination Hispanics experience in this country. In "Old Man," he honors his grandfather, who taught him to have pride in his heritage.

In the last poem, "Freeway 280" by Lorna Dee Cervantes, the speaker returns to her old neighborhood, which has been torn down and replaced by a highway. Amid the destruction, the speaker finds signs of life. Born in San Francisco in 1954, Cervantes has spent much of her time working with the Hispanic civil rights movement, known in the 1960s and 1970s as the Chicano movement. As a poet, she often explores the difficulties that arise from being caught between two cultures.

Bailando [1]

by Pat Mora

I will remember you dancing,
spinning round and round
a young girl in Mexico,
your long, black hair free in the wind,
spinning round and round
a young woman at village dances
your long, blue dress swaying
to the beat of *La Varsoviana*,[2]
smiling into the eyes of your partners,
years later smiling into my eyes
when I'd reach up to dance with you,
my dear aunt, who years later
danced with my children,
you, white-haired but still young
waltzing on your ninetieth birthday,
more beautiful than the orchid
pinned on your shoulder,
tottering now when you walk
but saying to me, *"Estoy*[3] *bailando,"*
and laughing.

---

1. **Bailando** (beye-LAHN-doh) *n.* dancing
2. *La Varsoviana* (lah vahr-soh-vee-AH-nah) an adaptation of a Polish
   polka
3. *Estoy* (ays-TOI) *v.* Spanish for *I am*

Old Man

by Ricardo Sánchez

remembrance (smiles/hurts sweetly)
October 8, 1972

old man
with brown skin
talking of past
    when being shepherd
    in utah, nevada, colorado and new mexico
was life lived freely;

old man,
  grandfather,
wise with time
running rivulets[1] on face,
deep, rich furrows,
  each one a legacy,
deep, rich memories
of life . . .
        "you are indio,[2]
          among other things,"
       he would tell me
         during nights spent
       so long ago
         amidst familial gatherings
       in albuquerque . . .
old man, loved and respected,
he would speak sometimes

---

1. **rivulets** (RIHV-yoo-lihts) *n. pl.* little streams
2. **indio** (EEN-dee-yoh) *adj.* Indian

of pueblos,[3]
      san juan, santa clara,
      and even santo domingo,
and his family, he would say,
came from there:
      some of our blood was here,
      he would say,
      before the coming of coronado,[4]
other of our blood
      came with los españoles,[5]
and the mixture
was rich,
      though often painful . . .

old man,
who knew earth
  by its awesome aromas
and who felt
the heated sweetness
  of chile verde[6]
by his supple touch,
gone into dust is your body
  with its stoic look and resolution,
but your reality, old man, lives on
in a mindsoul touched by you . . .

Old Man . . .

---

3. **pueblos** (PWEHB-lohz) *n. pl.* towns, villages; also people or nations. The reference here is to Native American pueblos in central and northern New Mexico.
4. **coronado** (koh-roh-NAH-doh) Francisco Vásquez de Coronado, Spanish explorer in the 1500s who led an expedition into what is now Arizona and New Mexico
5. **los españoles** (lohs ays-pahn-NYOHL-ays) *n. pl.* the Spaniards
6. **chile verde** (CHEE-lay VAIR-day) green pepper

Freeway 280

by Lorna Dee Cervantes

Las casitas[1] near the gray cannery,
nestled amid wild abrazos[2] of climbing roses
and man-high red geraniums
are gone now. The freeway conceals it
all beneath a raised scar.

But under the fake windsounds of the open lanes,
in the abandoned lots below, new grasses sprout,
wild mustard remembers, old gardens
come back stronger than they were,
trees have been left standing in their yards.
Albaricoqueros, cerezos, nogales . . .[3]
Viejitas[4] come here with paper bags to gather greens.
Espinaca, verdolagas, yerbabuena . . .[5]

I scramble over the wire fence
that would have kept me out.
Once, I wanted out, wanted the rigid lanes
to take me to a place without sun,
without the smell of tomatoes burning
on swing shift in the greasy summer air.

Maybe it's here
en los campos extraños de esta ciudad[6]
where I'll find it, that part of me
mown under
like a corpse
or a loose seed.

---

1. **Las casitas** (lahs kah-SEE-tahs) *n. pl.* the little houses
2. **abrazos** (ah-BRAH-zohs) *n. pl.* hugs, embraces
3. **Albaricoqueros, cerezos, nogales** (ahl-bah-ree-koh-KAY-rohs sair-AYS-ohs noh-GAH-lays) *n. pl.* apricot trees, cherry trees, walnut trees
4. **Viejitas** (vee-ay-HEE-tahs) *n. pl.* old women
5. **Espinaca, verdolagas, yerbabuena** (ays-pee-NAH-kah vair-doh-LAH-gahs YAIR-bah-BWAY-nah) *n.* spinach, purslane (an herb), and mint
6. **en los campos extraños de esta ciudad** (ayn lohs KAHM-pohs ayks-TRAHN-nyohs day AYS-tah see-yoo-DAHD) in the strange fields of this city

AFTER YOU READ

Exchanging Backgrounds and Cultures

1. In these three poems, the writers combine English with Spanish words and phrases. What does this suggest about the poets' attitudes toward their cultural identities?

2. How have the aunt in "Bailando" and the grandfather in "Old Man" influenced the speakers?

3. What do you think the speaker of "Freeway 280" hopes to find in her old neighborhood? Which lines in the poem best support your conclusion?

What Do You Think?

Which poem do you find most interesting? Why is it especially meaningful to you?

Experiencing Poetry

In "Bailando" and "Old Man," the speakers tell about their love and admiration for their relatives. Think about an older relative or friend who acts as a role model for you. Then, write a poem that shows your feelings for this person.

Optional Activity Write a poem in which you use a symbol to describe your feelings about a special place or object in your life. For example, in "Freeway 280," the freeway is a symbol that represents modern society, which has replaced an older, simpler way of life.

UNIT 3: FOCUS ON WRITING

Poems, like other forms of literature, convey messages through techniques such as imagery and figurative language. Like songs, poems have a musical quality that is created through repetition, rhythm, and rhyme.

Writing a Poem

Consider the following topics: a close friend, a personal achievement, a historical event, a social issue, or a favorite hobby. Then, write a poem about one of these topics or another topic of your choice.

The Writing Process

Good writing requires both time and effort. An effective writer completes a number of stages that together make up the writing process. The stages of the writing process are given below to help guide you through your assignment.

Prewriting

Once you have chosen a topic, develop a list of images, or word pictures, that relate to your topic. When you think of word pictures, remember the five senses: sight, hearing, touch, smell, and taste. For example, in her poem "Freeway 280," Lorna Dee Cervantes uses images such as the sound of the cars on the freeway, the smell of tomatoes burning, and the feeling of the greasy summer air. These images create clear pictures in the mind of the reader. When you have finished, review your lists and underline the most powerful or effective images.

Then, think about the theme you would like to express. The images should relate to the poem's theme. For example, in Alberto Ríos's poem "Nani," the elderly grandmother is described through images of serving food and speaking "through a hundred wrinkles."

Next, think about how you want your poem to sound. Do you want to use a regular rhythm or a pattern of accented syllables? Will you use rhyme? If so, list several words that rhyme with words on your list of images. Will you use other sound devices, such as alliteration?

Finally, think about the form of your poem. Where will the lines end? How many stanzas will there be? Will the stanzas be the same length?

Drafting and Revising

Draw from your list of images as you write. After every few lines, pause to read your poem aloud. Does it have the rhythm you wanted to create? Is the meaning clear?

When you have finished your first draft, read the entire poem aloud. Revise any lines or words that do not convey your desired sound or meaning.

You also may find it helpful to read your poem to a classmate. Use his or her comments to guide you in making revisions. Your classmate should refer to the following questions: Which are the most and the least effective images in the poem? How could they be made more vivid? Is the theme clear? If not, what could be done to make it clearer? How effective is the rhythm? What could be done to improve it?

Proofreading and Publishing

Now, proofread your final draft for errors in spelling, grammar, punctuation, and capitalization. Remember that some poems do not use standard punctuation and capitalization.

After you proofread your poem, you may want to read it aloud to your class. Try to read as expressively as possible, varying the tone and volume of your voice to show emotion and to emphasize important words. You also could send your poem to the school literary magazine or to a national student magazine such as *Merlin's Pen.*

DRAMA OF THE MEXICAN AMERICANS

Drama shares many elements with other forms of literature, but it is special because it is written to be seen and heard—to be performed. Whether a play is performed on stage or recorded on film, it brings actors and audiences together in a shared experience.

Drama also has a special written form. It is structured so that the setting, as well as the characters and their actions, emotions, and words, can be clearly understood by an audience. Notes about the setting and the characters' actions and emotions are called **stage directions**. These directions also include descriptions of the scenery that should appear on stage, the props or objects that actors may move or carry, and the kinds of lighting and sound effects that should be used during a performance. The words that each character speaks—the dialogue—are presented after the character's name.

Much as a novel often is divided into chapters, a play usually is divided into smaller sections. An **act** is a major section of a drama. Within an act, there are often smaller sections called **scenes**. The play you are about to read, *The Flying Tortilla Man*, is written as one long act with nine scenes.

Denise Chávez, the author of *The Flying Tortilla Man*, combines realism, fantasy, adventure, and humor in a tale that speaks to people of all ages. She weaves her views of life with aspects of her Mexican American culture and traditions. As you read, try to see the stage and hear the voices of the characters.

Fresco painted in April 1931 at Sigmund Stern home, Atherton, California. *Stern Hall, University of California, Berkeley.* Painting by Diego Rivera. Rivera was a well-known painter. He also was one of the leaders of the Mexican Mural Renaissance and received many mural commissions from corporations in the United States.

INTRODUCTION

The Flying
Tortilla Man

Writer and actress Denise Chávez was born in Las Cruces, New Mexico, in 1948. She has written that her earliest memories are of the extreme heat of New Mexico, the striking southwestern landscape, and the easygoing coexistence of Hispanic and mainstream cultures. These memories of growing up as a Mexican American in the small city of Las Cruces have greatly influenced her writing and acting.

Chávez's study of drama began at New Mexico State University. She received her Bachelor's degree in 1971 and went on to study at Trinity University, where she received a Master's degree in drama in 1974. She has had great success in performing one-woman shows across the southwestern United States and in writing and producing more than 20 plays. Chávez also has received recognition for her poetry and for *The Last of the Menu Girls*, a collection of short stories loosely based on her life. Her play *The Flying Tortilla Man* reflects her experiences and her heritage. As you will see, landscape and Mexican American history and culture are important elements in the play.

The Flying Tortilla Man

by Denise Chávez

"Beautiful or not, it is my native land. A relative or not, he is a fellow countryman."

Chinese Proverb

CHARACTERS

CARLOS	*age twelve*
NENO	*age twelve*
BENNIE	*age fourteen*
HERMANO GIL	*age forty-five*
ELIAS	*age thirteen*
BERTINA	*early fifties*
OSCAR	*age eighteen*
COTIL	*age fifteen*
TUDI	*age twenty*
FATTY CAMPBELL	*age fifty-five*
NORA	*early thirties*

THE BIRDS / OLD WOMEN

THE TORTILLA MAN   *ageless*

Scene 1

It is late evening on a hot summer night in Cuchillo,[1] New Mexico. The heat permeates the walls of an aluminum building that houses a small but prosperous tortilla factory. The odor of cooked maize hangs heavy in the air. The building seems collapsible, barely grounded to the earth. The factory is in full swing preparing for the day's orders. A screen door is held in place by two long wooden planks.

The radio jumps to a lively Mexican station, XELO, and casts a lyrical spell over the grinding, pulsating machines. Several teen-age boys are at their posts, silhouetted against machines in an eerie, yellow-maize darkness that creeps inside the factory and finds relief in the midst of activity.

Carlos *carries a pan of maize from a large metal trough to a machine that rinses the corn. He is a thin yet muscular boy of unspoiled character, gentle and filled with a natural goodness, a dreamer.* Carlos *stands not far from* Elias, *who supervises the maize in the grinding machine and changes the pans of crushed corn that go to the cutter as a finished masa.[2]* Elias *is a*

---

1. *Cuchillo* (koo-CHEE-yoh) *n.* The name means *knife.*
2. *masa* (MAH-sah) *n.* dough

mischievous adolescent with thick burnt red hair and fair skin, appropriately named "El Güero."[3] *Next to* Elias *stands* Neno, *guarding the cutting machines. He is about the same age as* Carlos, *somewhat tired and sickly-looking, with a dark chinless face. Not far from* Neno *stands* Bennie, *who pushes the dough through the cutting machine roller. He is silent and shy, lean and greyhoundlike.*[4] *At the end of the cooking conveyor belt sit* Oscar *and* Nora, *taking turns counting out a dozen tortillas and spreading them, fanlike, on the metal shelf where they are packaged by the roving* Bennie. Oscar *is fat, jolly and toothy.* Nora *is a cheerful woman, who is somewhat simple-minded, yet she works with amazing speed and agility.*

At the far end of the factory stands the office, a tucked-away bastion[5] *of power amid the heat and sweat. Inside is a large metal desk covered with orders and business papers. Beside the desk stands a counter full of frozen products from the factory: flour and corn tortillas, taco shells, tamales. At the desk, behind the closed and forbidding door, sits* Tudi, *who oversees the factory with a hard, anxious eye. He is a good-looking, somewhat morose young man. He is not the actual boss but simply manages the factory in the owner's stead. The radio plays . . . all are intense and involved in the swinging, swaying creation of the tortillas.*

Neno. It's hot!

Oscar. So, why don't you work in an ice plant?

Elias. Quiet, you guys, this is my favorite song!

Oscar (*laughing to himself*). This one, ese,[6] are you kidding me?

[*All are momentarily caught up in the dramatically sad tune coming from the radio: another song about lost love.*]

---

3. *El Güero* (ayl goo-WAY-roh) *n.* a fair-haired, light-skinned man
4. *greyhoundlike* (GRAY-hownd-leyek) *adj.* resembling a dog breed that is tall, slender, and swift
5. *bastion* (BASS-chuhn) *n.* a strongly defended or protected place
6. **ese** (AY-say) *n.* a slang term meaning *man* (you)

Neno. What am I doing here? I can't think . . . I can't breathe . . . it's so hot!

Oscar. You're not paid to think, man; you're paid to sweat!

Neno. I gotta get out of here . . . my head is on fire. Trade with me, Elias . . .

Elias. Heck no, Neno. I got my own work to do. You start doing it once, and you'll want to do it all the time.

Carlos. I'll trade, Neno.

Elias. They play this song to me this one night and you guys won't shut up.

Oscar. What's so special about tonight? It don't feel so special to me.

Elias. It's a special request from my girl!

Oscar. You have a girl, Güero? Who would want a pale worm like you?

Elias. None of your business, horsemouth!

Oscar. You called in the song yourself tonight, corn face, before you came in to work. Isn't that right, Nora? Doesn't have a girl at all, unless it's Nora here. Are you sweethearts with La Nica,[7] Elias? NicaNora, NicaNora, NicaNora, old metate[8] face. (Oscar *sings to* Nora, *who is first oblivious to him and then joins in, clapping her hands and humming, in a strange and haunting way.* Neno *is beginning to look progressively worse, and* Elias *makes ugly scowling faces at* Oscar, *who encourages* Bennie *to join him in his crazed chanting.*) NicaNora, NicaNora, NicaNora, old metate face! Laugh, Nica, laugh!

Elias. You're jealous!

Oscar. Of La Nica? Heck, man, I see her every day—that's enough for me.

Nora. Funny, Oscar, funny! (Nora *continues to clap her hands.*)

---

7. **La Nica** (lah NEE-kah) a nonsense name given to Nora by Oscar
8. **metate** (may-TAH-tay) *adj.* a flat stone slab used to grind corn

Oscar. Be quiet, Nora, and get back to work! The Boss gonna get on our case. We got lots of work to do . . .

[Nora *hums*.]

Carlos. Nora hasn't done anything to you, Oscar; leave her alone!

Oscar. *You* leave *me* alone, Mr. Corn Lifter. I was only making fun.

Elias. You tell him, Carlos . . . trying to make believe that La Nica is my girlfriend. That old hag, I'd rather drown in the irrigation ditch!

Carlos. Leave her alone, Elias!

Oscar. But she's his ruca,[9] ese . . .

Elias. If you're such a good boy, Carlos, be quiet . . . shut your mouth, okay?

Carlos. Where's Tudi? He's been gone a long time. I'm worried about Neno.

Nora. Tudi? Tudi?

Oscar. Shut up and get to work!

Carlos. Don't talk to her that way, Oscar. Show some respect!

Oscar. To a crazy woman?

Elias. You think you're so good, Carlos . . . well, you're the one that's crazy! That's what happens when you don't have real parents. When you're an orphan! And when you live with people that ain't your kin, in a house full of strangers!

Carlos. I have parents!

Elias. You call those two—the stringbean and the squash—your parents? Heck, man, they have a houseful of kids, like rabbits, over there at that place.

Carlos. They're good to me.

Elias. It's because they feel sorry.

Nora. Carlitos, good boy!

Elias. See, even La Nica feels sorry.

---

9. ruca (ROO-kah) *n.* slang for *girlfriend*

Oscar. Go on Elias; you're finally showing a little nerve. Nica might fall in love with your strength!

Bennie. You guys better be still. Tudi might come back!

Oscar. Let him come back. I'll show him who OSCAR SALCEDO is!

Elias. Híjole,[10] Oscar, you couldn't whip a mouse!

Oscar. Be careful, you bleached earthworm!

Elias. You're going to get it one of these days, you fat hyena!

Bennie. Be quiet! Be quiet, or we'll get in trouble! Tudi's in his office!

Oscar. So El Tudi is in the office, huh? I don't trust that guy. He always looks like a dog who wants to bark. Too much power. Wooo! What do you say, Nica?

Nora. Where's Tudi? Tudi is a nice man.

Carlos. Her name is Nora.

Oscar (*referring to* Nora *as he counts tortillas*). So what does she know anyway? All she can do is count to twelve. Ay, this heat! It gets into your blood and drives you crazy. After so many years, you start counting all the time. Stupid things you start counting for nothing. All this heat . . . it affects your brain. It starts suddenly, like with Neno, until one day you're as dry in the head as Nica, right, Nenito? Where'd he go?

Carlos. He's at the washer.

Bennie. Don't let Tudi see you, Neno; it'll go rough for us!

Elias. So who cares! You've all got baked corn for brains, anyway!

Neno. I don't feel good. I'm going outside. (Neno *starts for the door and suddenly faints.* Carlos, Elias, *and* Bennie *run to him, followed by* Nora. Oscar *remains behind.*)

Oscar (*paying no attention to the others, he continues talking*). You just keep counting, that's all . . .

Carlos. What's wrong, Neno?

---

10. Híjole (EE-ho-lay) *int.* (slang) Gosh!

Bennie. He's sick!

Elias. You're really a smart one, Bennie. Is that why you work here?

Bennie. What about you, Güero? The light too bright for you out there in the world? You need to be in this cave, eh?

Oscar (*still oblivious to the others,* Oscar *continues to count tortillas*). Ten . . . eleven . . . twelve . . .

Carlos. Help me take him outside. He needs some fresh air.

Oscar. He's got the rot. It just happens.

Elias. You must be an advanced case.

Oscar. Sooner or later. . .

Elias. Would you shut up?

Oscar. It gets you.

Elias. Is that why you're still here after all these years?

[*The boys carry* Neno *outside and lean him up against the steps.* Nora *has gone to the water trough near the maize bags and dips her apron in and returns to the steps. She uses her apron as a towel on* Neno's *forehead.* Neno *is in a daze.*]

Carlos. Thank you, Nora.

Nora (*in a soothing voice*). Neno, Nenito. Good boy, Nenito.

[Neno *unsteadily gets to his feet with the help of Nora and Carlos.*]

Elias. Oh, he's okay.

[Bennie, Elias, Carlos, Nora *and* Neno *file back inside the building.*]

Bennie. We'd better get back to work!

Oscar. Since when have you worked around here, Bennie? And you, Nica. Where have you been, you lazy good-for-nothing? Who do you think you are, wiping people's foreheads? And who does Neno think he is? Hey, I already did more than my share of work, so where is everybody?

[Nora *runs back, confused. Her movements are pointed and jittery.*]

Nora. Sorry, Nora so sorry. Oscar not mad with Nora. She's sorry.

Oscar. Back to work, back to work! They can hear you in the other room, the bosses, the big shots. They can hear you out here like rats in the night. Isn't that right, Nica, like rats?

Nora (*making a ratlike face*). Like rats, like rats.

Carlos. Leave her alone, Oscar . . . she hasn't done anything to you. She was only trying to help Neno out.

Oscar. It'll go bad for us all, Carlos. You get back to work.

Carlos. He's sick!

Oscar. He's got the corn rot and the fever that comes nights working at a place like this. It starts flowing in your blood.

Elias (*sarcastically*). What are you anyway, a doctor?

Oscar. And you're the nurse!

Carlos. I can't leave him alone. He's sick!

Oscar. Oh, that's right . . . you're the one who doesn't have anyone to take care of you, so you take care of the world.

Tudi (*coming in and looking around suspiciously*). What's going on? Why aren't you working?

Neno. I'll be okay in a few minutes.

Bennie. Didn't I tell you guys?

Tudi. Get to work! All of you!

Carlos. Neno isn't feeling well, Tudi, I . . .

Tudi. Get to work, Carlos. We have orders to fill. It's late. The night's almost over and we're behind. Go on, all of you!

Carlos. Neno is sick. He needs to rest. Maybe he should go home.

Tudi. We can't have this, Carlos. We have orders to fill. This isn't the first time someone has played a trick, pretending to be sick . . .

Carlos. Feel his head . . .

Tudi. Huerfanito,[11] you, Carlos . . . help Neno get back to his job. He'll make it, all right. Now, boys, I've been in the office, thinking. (Oscar *snickers.*) And I've come up with a new set of rules.

Oscar. Not again!

Tudi. Quiet! Number one: one break every three hours, depending how far behind we are. Number two: no eating or drinking on the job. Number three: no visiting of an extended nature.

Oscar. Number four: No breathing! Visiting, man, are you joking me? Who's there to visit en esta maldita cueva?[12]

Tudi. Number four: more than one absence constitutes dismissal. Number five: we will all work together as a happy, united working force, producing as best as we can, without strife and dissension.[13]

Bennie. Dissension, what's dissension?

Tudi. Quiet! Now then, I'll be available to talk to you guys any time. Remember that I'm the boss in place of our BOSS, who is gone. I am the absolute head in his place, and I demand respect and will treat your accordingly. Come on, boys, let's be friends!

Oscar. After all that . . . man, are you pulling my leg? It's a joke, Tudi.

Carlos. I'm taking Neno home, Tudi.

Elias. Let them go, let them go. . .they're nothing but trouble.

Oscar. Those two didn't do a thing all night.

Nora. Nice boys, Tudi, they're my friends.

Tudi. La Nica's very talkative tonight. She seems to be on

---

11. **Huerfanito** (wair-fah-NEE-toh) *n.* little orphan
12. **en esta maldita cueva** (ayn AY-stah mahl-DEE-tah KWAY-vah) in this accursed cave
13. **dissension** (dih-SEN-shuhn) *n.* disagreement or violent quarreling

your side, Carlos. Why are you helping Neno anyway? You know none of them would ever lift a finger for you. You could die right here on the job.

Oscar. Carlos was just standing around doing nothing, Tudi.

Carlos. I was helping my friend. I'm taking him home.

Tudi. If you do that, you might not have a job when you get back.

Carlos. You just can't *not* help someone. Especially a friend, someone you work with. Look at him, Tudi . . . he looks bad. Friendship is more than just standing by while someone is sick. Neno and I are friends.

Tudi. Go on, Carlos. Get outta here. Just try and come back. You're always getting in my way. Take your friend home. Just take him home. He's worthless!

Neno. I'm feeling better; really, I am. I can go to work, Carlos. I can go . . . (*He appears ready to faint and then recovers a bit.*) I can go home alone, Carlos; you stay here. Let me go alone.

Carlos. I'm taking you home! I care more about you than all the tortillas in the world!

Elias. Ah, they'll be back, begging for a job!

Tudi. Just you wait and see what happens, Carlos. Go on with you! Don't come back!

Nora. Goodbye. Goodbye, my friends. See you soon.

Oscar. You make me laugh, Nica. You really make me laugh! (*He starts laughing. They all join in.* Carlos *and* Neno *exit.*)

[*It is a rainy, windy night. The lightning crackles the breeze, and the boys look small and helpless against the sky. They don't have too far to go to* Neno's *but they make their way slowly and cautiously, pausing under the archways and porches, huddling together against the fury of the oncoming storm.* Carlos *knocks at* Neno's *door. A women answers and takes* Neno *in, then closes the door.* Carlos *stands there long after they have gone in, unsure of what to do. He then dashes out of the doorway and runs madly to the next shelter. A delicate-looking man of above-average height with a fine, smooth face and warm, small eyes is standing there, also seeking shelter. They look at one another for a few seconds, the boy and the man, both dreamers.*]

Tortilla Man. Where are you, boy?

[Carlos *is not sure he heard the old gentleman correctly. He is taken aback by the seemingly strange question. Often* The Tortilla Man *will ask questions that seem to make no sense whatsoever, and yet they really do.*]

Carlos (*in an uncertain voice*). Where am I going, sir?

Tortilla Man. Where are you?

Carlos. I don't understand.

Tortilla Man. That's what's wrong with everyone. They're out of touch; they don't know where they are, especially in the middle of a storm. They're lost, going from one place to another, from one thing to another.

Carlos. WHO are you?

Tortilla Man. You don't know me?

Carlos (*suddenly wary*). What do you want?

Tortilla Man. What makes you think I want anything?

Carlos. If you'll excuse me, sir, I'll have to leave you and get back to work.

Tortilla Man. If I were you, I'd stay around and talk awhile. It's too early to be running off, and besides, your Boss hasn't decided to take you back yet. Wait up, boy; talk to an old man . . . tell him where you are.

Carlos. Who are you? You seem to know a lot. You're not from here, are you?

Tortilla Man. I remember Cuchillo when there was nothing out here but rocks and weeds and the bare sky to wear as a hat . . . when you blessed yourself for another day in this wilderness and prayed for rain . . .

Carlos. You don't look *that* old . . .

Tortilla Man. No impudence, boy, just listen to me. For he who teaches you for one day is your father for life. I read that in a book.

Carlos. I can barely read, and I don't have a father.

Tortilla Man. You do now, boy. We're in the same line of work.

Carlos. Tortillas?

Tortilla Man. Well, yes and no. Mostly yes.

Carlos. I don't have a job now. I've been fired. I don't know whether I should go back and beg—they said I would—or whether I should go home . . . I mean, where I live. My parents, Hermano Gil[14] and Bertina, they'll be mad at me. I finally got this job and now it's gone!

Tortilla Man. You'll go back to the factory, of course. No one should ever avoid what needs to be done.

Carlos. Yes, I thought so, too. How did you know?

Tortilla Man. We do the same work.

Carlos. You make tortillas, too?

Tortilla Man. In a way, yes, but we'll come to that later. We both make things grow, come alive.

Carlos. We do?

Tortilla Man. We do, Carlos!

Carlos. You know my name!

Tortilla Man. Boy, you look like a Carlos—long, gangly, a real weed, a Carlos who is growing.

Carlos. You talk funny!

Tortilla Man. Boy, you look funny, all wet and long!

[*They both laugh.*]

Carlos. Who are you?

Tortilla Man. I'm The Flying Tortilla Man.

Carlos. The Tortilla Man? You run a factory, like our boss? He's never there, so Tudi takes his place. I never have seen the boss; I don't even know who he is . . .

Carlos (*realizing* The Tortilla Man *might be his boss*). You aren't . . .

---

14. **Hermano Gil** (air-MAH-noh HEEL) Brother Gil; *brother* is a term of respect.

Tortilla Man. I make things grow.

Carlos. But tortillas don't grow! They're a dead thing . . . they're just corn that becomes bread and that's eaten and is gone . . .

Tortilla Man. But, Carlos, tortillas are more than that . . . they're life to so many people. They're magic offerings; they're alive as the land, and as flat!

Carlos. They are, huh? What's your real name?

Tortilla Man. Juan.

Carlos. You're Mr. Juan, The Tortilla Man; pleased to meet you.

Tortilla Man. Enchanted. We are enchanted to meet you.

Carlos. Who's we?

Tortilla Man. Why, the Magic Tortilla, of course.

Carlos (*looking around*). Where is it?

Tortilla Man (*putting his arm around* Carlos's *shoulder and speaking confidentially*). I couldn't bring it out in this rain, could I?

Carlos (*disappointed*). I guess not.

Tortilla Man. Now . . . back to work . . . they're waiting for you.

Carlos. They are?

Tortilla Man. Don't be impudent, boy . . . don't you trust me?

Carlos. Yes . . . yes, I do! But I know I don't have a job anymore.

Tortilla Man. Who says? You just wait and see. Carlos, you just wait and see. You just can't stop something from growing.

Carlos. I'll try . . . I'll try . . .

Tortilla Man. Grow, boy. Let them see you grow, in front of their eyes! (*He laughs an infectious, clear laugh that is warm and comforting.*) You'll see. It's waiting there to grow . . . they can't stop you. They can't stop you . . . they'll try . . . Now, goodbye, think of me, and run, run . . .

[Carlos *runs into the darkness of a now-clear night. He is full of energy. He suddenly stops to say something to* The Tortilla Man, *who has vanished.*]

Carlos. THANK YOU! Sir . . . Mr. Juan . . . goodbye . . . he says he makes things grow, but how? Magic tortillas? And he says the sky is a hat . . .

[Carlos *runs back to the factory and walks in. Everyone is working noisily. The radio competes with the tortilla machine for dominance.*]

Tudi (*seeing* Carlos, *he signals for him to come closer*). It's about time . . . what took you so long?
Carlos. I was getting some fresh air; it's too hot in here . . .
Oscar. There, what'd I tell you . . . the rot . . . it starts nights . . .
Elias. Shut up!!
Tudi. Well, get back to work! We have orders to fill and the night is half over, and we've just begun!
Oscar. You're lucky, man . . . you're just lucky. Isn't that right, Nica?
Nora. Hello, Carlitos. Hello. How's your Mama?
Oscar. What a memory!
Nora. Lucky boy, lucky boy.
Carlos (*back at his post, he rinses out the maize*). I'm fine, Nora . . . I'm just fine! How are you?

[*Blackout. End of scene one.*]

Scene 2

The orphanage where Carlos *lives with his foster parents,* Hermano Gil *and* Bertina. *It is a large, rambling house with about twenty-five children and teen-agers and two frazzled adults. The orphans are not juvenile delinquents, merely displaced and disoriented people.* Carlos's *room is set off from the main house. It is a small junk-filled closet/shed that serves as a storage area and utility room, as well as* Carlos's *room. Spread about the room are boxes full of cloth remnants, paper, old toys, and empty luggage; up against the wall, near* Carlos's *bed, are some old picture frames, an old hoe, and some posters, as well as a beat-up, much-used vacuum cleaner. Nonetheless, despite its disarray, the room has a certain personal coziness, as if someone has tried his best to make a living space of his own and half succeeded. There is a small night table next to the bed and a chest of drawers nearby. On the table is an old decorated cigar box, with CARLOS written on the outside. It is* Carlos's *private property and personal joy. Inside the box are an old dried feather, a small fossil, a large rubber band tied into a series of amazing knots, a soft red handkerchief, two glass marbles, and a picture of a sickly old woman in black. It is a picture of Isa,* Carlos's *guardian after the death of his mother, whom he hardly knew.* Carlos *is sleeping. It is about six a.m. He has not been in bed very long. A man is singing. It is* Hermano Gil. *He is a short, smallish man who works in the kitchen of a Mexican restaurant. He is energetic and sprightly despite the hour and his obvious inebriation. He has a dark complexion that seems even darker in the half-light.*

The house is asleep for the most part, and the lights have a dim, early-morning quality. Carlos *sleeps in a twisted position. Suddenly, the door opens to his room, and his foster father,* Hermano Gil, *wanders in, looking for something in the dark room. He accidentally falls against the sleeping* Carlos. Hermano Gil *gets up and continues his search for a suitcase of his that is somewhere in the room.*

Hermano Gil. This is the last time I'll bother you, any one of you . . . this time I'm leaving for good! I'll take a job as a singer. (*He sings a few bars from a Mexican love ballad in Spanish.*) I'll come up in the world at last. Half my life spent in someone else's kitchen, cleaning up. That's no kind of life. Then I have to come home to a house full of strangers. I told Bertina, "Don't do it, Bert." I said, "I can't take it." She didn't listen. "I can't be a father to the entire world; we have a daughter of our own. Isn't that enough, woman? I'm leaving . . . I'm leaving . . . "

Carlos (*he has awakened and is sitting up on the bed, listening*). Papa, wait, don't leave!

Hermano Gil. I'm not your Papa . . . let me pack.

Carlos (*in a tired and sleepy voice*). We'll miss you, Papa!

Hermano Gil. I have to leave. I can't go on living in a hallway in a house full of lost children. What am I talking about? I just work in a kitchen. (*looking at Carlos*) You're nothing to me!

Carlos. Don't say that, Papa. We love you!

Hermano Gil. All my life in a kitchen . . . for what? To run a house for stray dogs and cats . . . all my money going to feed twenty-five hungry mouths . . . as if Bertina and Cotil and I didn't have our own problems.

[Hermano Gil *sits down on the edge of the bed. He puts his hand on the side of his head and sighs. He is holding a ragged suitcase. As* Hermano Gil *is bemoaning his fate, he accidentally knocks over* Carlos's *cigarbox, and the contents fall to the floor.* Carlos *scrambles to retrieve the objects, but* Hermano Gil *has swooped them up and holds them in his dark and unsteady hands.*]

Carlos. Papa!

Hermano Gil. So why do you keep this junk? Isn't there enough here already to crowd into your life?

Carlos. These are *my* things—they mean something to *me!* They remind me of people and places and times I've loved. They're alive to me.

Hermano Gil. This seashell is dead, son. There was a life here once, but where is it now? Show me, if you can. Can it talk to you? Can it tell you how it feels to be buried in the sand and come up to the sky as a rock, a hardened thing, an outline of something that was once alive? No, son, these are dead things—they have no use. You keep them because you are a silly dreamer like I used to be and because you make up stories to pass away your silly time. Like how you are going to be a singer and come up in the world . . . (*Referring to his own broken life,* Hermano Gil *breaks down and cries.* Carlos *comforts him.* Hermano Gil *wipes his eyes and looks at the knots in the rubber band.*) This game of knots, this game of glass. Of what use is it? (*He cries a bit more and then looks at the picture.*) Who is this old pan face? She has the skin of an old wrinkled prune . . . This is what I mean, Carlitos! Your name is Carlos; I forget with all the names. I forget, son, so many people pass through here and go away with not so much as a thank you for the food. They leave their mugres[15]—stuff, son, stuff—behind for us to collect and store in this room. (*He looks at the feather and the rock.*) What is this? What does this mean? This dirty old bird feather and this rock?

Carlos. It's not a rock, Papa; it's a fossil.

Hermano Gil. It's a dirty old rock and this is a chicken feather! Like the ones whose necks I used to wring when I was a boy . . . (*He imitates the wringing of a chicken's neck.*) Squawk!

Carlos. It's a seashell.

Hermano Gil. So it is, Juanito.

Carlos. Carlos, Papa . . . Let me have my things, please, Papa . . . please.

Hermano Gil (*referring to the photograph*). This is the deadest thing of all, in black, like a spider.

Carlos. That's Isa, my mother's aunt. She took care of me when Mama died.

Hermano Gil (*touched*). Here, son . . . (*He puts the objects on the bed.*) Keep your treasures. You may be a fool, but you have a heart, and no man—not even the worst of us—can go against that. Keep your treasures. You'll need them out there in the world. Keep your feathers, your rocks, and your old lady's knotted life. (*He gets up.*) I don't want

---

15. **mugres** (MOO-grays) *n.* junk

anything to do with strangers anymore. You've worn me out. I'm tired of trying to feed and clothe the world.

[Carlos *takes his things and puts them back in the box. Then he goes to the chest of drawers and puts the box on top of it, under some clothing, just as* Cotil *comes in.* Cotil *is a conniving young lady of fifteen, who besides being prone to fits of unthinking and unsolicited malice, is a chubby romantic.*]

Cotil. Hiding things again, lazy boy?

Carlos. Good morning, Cotil.

Cotil. Papa, Mama wants you to get ready for work.

Hermano Gil. I told you, I'm leaving. This is it, Cotil. You're the only flesh and blood of mine in this infernal household. Why should I remain the father of this faceless screaming brood? Tell me!

Cotil. Mama wants you to come and eat, or the atole[16] will get cold.

Hermano Gil. EAT? Child, how can I eat the fruit of my labor with a mouth full of sand? Let the maggots take it!

Cotil. Papa, you better go before Mama comes to get you. And you, lazy boy, get up. You've already slept long enough.

Hermano Gil. Leave him alone.

Cotil. If I do, Papa, he'll sleep all day.

Hermano Gil. He's one of the few people that works around here. Let him rest! Go away!

Cotil. I'll tell Mama!

Hermano Gil. Tell her . . . tell her!

Cotil. You'd better get up, Carlos. I'll tell Mama you steal and hide things. I'll show her where you put them.

Hermano Gil. Out, out!

Cotil. He's got you believing him. Papa!

Hermano Gil. Flesh of my flesh, blood of my blood . . . (Cotil *exists with a wicked smile.* Hermano Gil *rises and gets ready to go to breakfast.*) Can you put away the suitcase,

---

16. atole (ah-TOH-lay) *n.* hot corn gruel

Carlitos? I am a bit hungry, now that I think about it. Carlos, you and me, we'll go away someday, just the two of us, just the two of us old fossils and we'll never come back . . .

Bertina (*yelling from the kitchen*). Gil, honey, come on. Come and have breakfast, or you'll be late for work.

Hermano Gil (*speaking to* Carlos). We'll have to make a few plans before we can leave . . . I'm coming . . . I'm coming, Bert!

Carlos. I'm sorry, Papa; I'll help you. I'll go away and become rich, and I'll send you lots of money. I'll make you happy.

Hermano Gil. Ha! Go back to bed and dream some more, son. Rub your magic things together and pray for someone to show you the way. Ask for money first, then loaves of bread and fish. Pray for rain, boy. This is New Mexico and our souls are dry! No, boy, go back to bed, but first put up the suitcase, so I'll know where to find it the next time . . . Thanks, son . . . (Hermano Gil *pauses in the doorway.*) It's so nice, so nice to believe in miracles . . . so keep your dried-out turkey feathers, who knows . . . who really knows . . .

[Bertina *is at the door, with* Cotil *beside her.* Bertina *is in her early fifties, a plump, kindly woman who is gracious and tactful.*]

Cotil. I told you, Mama. I told you they were talking and plotting, making all kinds of plans. Carlos is a troublemaker, Mama. I've always told you that.

Hermano Gil. Hello, Bert. Good morning to my dear and beloved wife and darling daughter.

Cotil. Carlos is a snake, Mama!

Hermano Gil. Shut up, my darling girl. Now go run and sharpen your tongue while your Mama and I eat breakfast.

Bertina. Go on, Cotil; your father is hungry.

Cotil. But MAMA!

Bertina. I only say things once. You know that. What would you like for breakfast, Gilito?

Hermano Gil. I thought you decided already. You take care of things like that, Bert. You always do.

Bertina. We'll start with a little atole . . . chile . . . (*They exit.*)

Cotil. What about Carlos? He's still in bed, Mama!

Hermano Gil. Let the world sleep! I'm going to have my atolito. You have all day to run your mother ragged, Cotil. I don't know how she does it. I don't know how you do it, Bert. A house full of children, both young and old.

Bertina. I love them as I love you, Gilito . . . that's all. We're all God's children . . .

Hermano Gil. But twenty-five!!

Cotil (*standing at the door to* Carlos's *room*). I saw you hide that box, Carlitos Warlitos. Such a good boy wouldn't have secrets.

Carlos. I don't!

Cotil. Then show me what's in the box!

Carlos. They're personal things.

Cotil. Nothing is personal in this house.

Carlos. Let me sleep!

Cotil. You're a lazy orphan, and my Mama and Papa don't really love you. They only put up with you because you don't have parents or a house.

Carlos. Leave me alone . . . please, Cotil.

Cotil. I'll never leave you alone—never!

Carlos. You hate me, don't you?

Cotil. Yes! You orphan!

Carlos (*sitting on the bed*). Why? Why? I haven't done anything to you!

Cotil. You think you're better than us.

Carlos. No, I don't!

Cotil. You have secrets!

Carlos. Why do you hate me so much, Cotil? (*It is a tense, electric moment.*)

Cotil. I don't know . . . but I do! (*She slams the door and leaves. She thinks twice about it and returns.*) Get up, you lazy, yawning nobody, or I'll tell Mama about your secrets!

[Cotil *exits and leaves* Carlos *very hurt and stunned.*]

Carlos. What have I done that everyone hates me? I'm quiet and I work hard and all they do is yell at me. Get to work! Get to work! You better straighten up and show respect! I don't understand. Who can tell me what's going wrong? (Carlos *goes to the chest of drawers and removes the box from underneath the clothing. He looks at the photograph and then at the fossil.*) Hello, Isa. What can you tell me today? Gone to see some friends? And you, Carlos, do you have any friends? (*Thinking aloud,* Carlos *remembers* Mr. Juan.) Where are you now, Mr. Juan? (*remembering* The Tortilla Man's *words*) He said they'll try and stop you. They'll try but they can't . . . because for some reason, a person wants to keep growing . . . (Carlos *goes back to sleep.*)

Scene 3

*E*arly *the next evening, outside the factory. The workers have not yet arrived. We can hear whispers in the distance.*

Elias. I'm here behind the building. To the right. Did you have any trouble?

Cotil. I had to sneak out of the house.

Elias. Will you get into trouble?

Cotil. Oh, no! I can do just about anything and my Mama won't care. She likes me. I'm the favorite.

Elias. What about your Papa?

Cotil. What about him? He does what my Mama says.

Elias (*coming closer to* Cotil, *he puts his arms around her*). Cotil, how are you?

Cotil (*moving away*). We don't have much time. Is everything ready?

Elias. Yes, Cotil. Oscar and I have gone over the plans many times. There's no doubt that we'll get Carlos—and good this time. Who does he think he is, walking all over Oscar and me like we were rocks under his feet?

Cotil. He's that way. He needs to be taught a lesson. He strolls through our house like he owns it, like he was my own true brother.

Elias. I'm glad I'm not your brother! Why don't you stay awhile?

Cotil. I have to go or Mama will get suspicious. You see, lucky for us, Carlos left the house to do an errand for Papa, and I snuck into his room and got this . . . (*She brings* Carlos's *cigar box from behind her back and shows it to* Elias.) See, it says CARLOS on it. That way, when the robbery is reported, everyone will figure he stole the stuff.

Elias. I'm glad you came, my dove, my little sunshine.

Cotil. Let's get on with it, okay?

Elias. Okay, Okay. This is the plan: after work we stick around, Oscar and I. He opens the locks—he's real good at that—then we go into the office and fool around the safe. We mess up the room and leave. When Tudi comes in tomorrow morning, he sees Carlos's box and he figures out who broke in.

Cotil. Are you sure it'll work?

Elias. Aren't I Elias Macias? Hey, babe, by tomorrow Carlos will be fired. We'll have put him in his place. It's taken time to settle accounts with that goody-goody. Say, babe, can't you stay awhile?

Cotil. I have to get home. I just wanted to make sure everything is going okay.

Elias. Will you think of me?

Cotil. I do every night, Elias, just before I go to sleep.

Elias. Really?

Cotil. Yeah, now go on . . . listen to the radio . . . for a sign from me . . .

Elias. Cotil, the guys don't believe I have a girlfriend. How come you don't want to go out with me in public? (Cotil *looks away from him with an annoyed expression.*) Well, okay . . . until tomorrow. We'll celebrate the downfall of that plaster saint. There's no one worse than someone who smiles a lot with phony goodness . . . Goodnight, Cotil.

Cotil. Goodbye. Make sure that all goes well. (*She exits.*)

Elias. My Cotil . . . will you dedicate a song for me tonight? Ay! (*He sighs and exits with* Carlos's *box.*)

[*It is now about eight p.m. Everyone starts to arrive. By the side of the road stand four old women in black, who later become* The Birds, Tin, Tan, Ton, *and* Mabel.]

Woman One (*referring to the boys coming in for work at the tortilla factory*). Those boys, it's disgraceful . . .

Woman Two. Where is he?

Woman Three. Who?

Woman Four. The boy.

Woman Two. I don't see him.

Woman One. The rascally thin one, over there, over there.

Woman Four. His parents were killed when he was nothing . . .

Woman One. He was very small, wrinkled from his mother . . .

Woman Three. Full of his father's sweat . . .

Woman Two. They were killed?

Woman Four. He's always been alone, like the sore on the side of the mouth, turned inside with a life of its own . . .

Woman One. There he goes . . .

Woman Two. Who?

Woman Four. He's all alone . . .

Woman Three. The boy . . .

[*The boys come up.* Tudi *is the first to arrive. He opens up the tortilla factory, turns on the lights and the machines.* Bennie *and* Oscar *are behind him, followed by* Carlos *and* Elias. Nora *wanders in last.* Elias *is carrying a paper bag with the cigar box inside. He and* Oscar *wink to each other.*]

Tudi. Hello, boys!

All. Hello, Tudi!

Carlos. How are you, Tudi?

Tudi. I just said hello.

Nora. Hello, hello. I'm fine.

Tudi. I'm ready for work. How about everyone else?

[*Various grumbles, moans, sighs, and a belch can be heard.*]

124

Oscar. I'm ready to go out on the town, to do anything but slave in this furnace.

Elias (*looking at* Oscar). We'll have to set off some fireworks later on, eh, Oscar? Won't we?

Tudi. What's this? All of a sudden two fighting dogs become friends. It must be the end of the world.

Elias. We've come to an understanding.

Oscar. Some common ground.

Tudi. Probably some common hate. Don't forget about rule number three: socializing too much.

Oscar. Oh, yes, sir, Mr. Tudi.

Nora. Hello, hello, hello. I'm fine.

Tudi. Okay, okay, let's get to work. (*Talking to* Oscar) Are you setting up, Oscar?

Elias. Yes, we've got it all worked out . . . right, Oscar?

Tudi. Ready, Carlos . . . Nora?

Nora. Ready, Tudi, ready.

Carlos. I'm glad to see you and Oscar have become friends, Elias.

Tudi. Something must be wrong.

Elias. Finally something is right. We discovered a way to settle old debts.

Tudi. Get to work, you bums. We've been here ten minutes and you haven't done a bit of work. Hurry up there, Nora!

Nora. Okay, Tudi, I hurry.

Oscar. Here it comes, folks . . . THE TORTILLA EXPRESS!!

[*The action is speeded up. The machines roar, night goes by. Suddenly, it is early morning and the work is done.* Tudi *is beginning to turn off the lights and lock up.*]

Elias. Hey, Oscar, did you hear about Neno?

Oscar. What happened, man?

Elias. You were right.

Tudi. You guys must really be sick. Are you actually agreeing with him, Elias?

Elias. Neno's got the corn rot.

Oscar. He does?

Carlos. What's this, Elias? What's wrong?

Elias. Neno's got the rot. He's in bed. He's really sick. They don't know if he's going to make it.

Tudi. He was always sickly. The first time I saw him he looked like a stale sausage, very dark with bloody eyes. He was never healthy.

Oscar. I've said it again and again . . . it'll get you sooner or later. It gets into your blood after awhile and then there's no going back. You're lost.

Carlos. Neno is really sick? We should go see him.

Elias. Not me! I might get the rot from being near him.

Oscar. He was never a friend of mine. Too puny and dark.

Elias. I never knew him that well.

Nora. Nora all finished with work. She go home.

Carlos. I'll walk you, Nora.

Oscar. Uuucheee, it's too funny!

Elias. They're sweethearts, Oscar!

Tudi. Get out of here, you worms! I haven't got all day to put up with a bunch of lazy, rascally caterpillars. I have to lock up.

Carlos (*speaking gently to* Nora). Neno's sick.

Nora. Where's Nenito?

Oscar. Why do you bother with her? She can't understand you. One . . . two . . . three . . . four . . . five . . . six . . . seven . . . eight . . . nine . . . ten . . . eleven . . . twelve—that's all she understands. The two of you keep trying to make sense, and no one can understand.

Carlos. Let's go, Nora.

Nora. Goodbye, my friends.

Tudi. Go on, I have my work to do.

Carlos. Have a nice day, Tudi!

Tudi. Haven't you left yet?

Elias. I'm going.

Tudi. Well, hurry up!

Elias. Bye, you guys.

Carlos. Bye, Elias.

Elias (*to* Oscar). Hey, man, I'll walk with you.

Tudi. So goodbye already . . . this must be the end of the world.

Oscar. Let's go.

[*They exit and disappear around the building. They wait until* Tudi *has locked up and has gone.* Carlos *and* Nora *have left.* Oscar *and* Elias *emerge from the shadows and furtively slip into the doorway.* Oscar *begins fiddling with the door lock.*]

Elias. Where'd you learn that?

Oscar. You think I've been making tortillas all my life? I'm a T.V.I.[17] graduate.

Elias. I never knew you were so smart, Oscar.

Oscar. Haven't I told you all this time?

Elias. But who listens?

Oscar. Did Cotil come?

Elias. She gave me something that will put our Carlos in real trouble. See, it's a box with his name on it. When we get inside the office, we'll drop it on the floor for Tudi to find. It's all settled. We'll get him yet!

[*They go inside quietly. Once they open the office door, they rummage around the room, dropping the box, and then leave as quietly and as quickly as possible. While they have been doing this,* Nora *has returned, looking for* Neno. *She sees what is going on but does not fully comprehend its significance. She slips away. Meanwhile,* Carlos *has returned to wait for* The Tortilla Man *under the same stoop. He is tired and sleepy. He sits back, leaning up against the door, and falls into a heavy sleep. He hears the sounds of voices, then a solitary voice—first far away, then near. It is a soothing, melodious voice, the type one hears in dreams. It has a sweet clarity and richness that comes from a height and flows past the dreamer until it is there beside him.* Carlos *feels a*

---

17. T.V.I. Technical and Vocational Institute

coolness and a movement but is unsure of where he is. Suddenly he feels a warm tingling sensation on his face. Carlos *is startled and jumps up. This sudden movement jars him out of the dream. He is now awake.*]

Carlos. Where am I? (*Although he finds himself in mid-air, on a smooth disc, he is reassured to see* The Tortilla Man.)

Tortilla Man. Don't be impudent, boy. Where do you think you are?

Carlos. Where am I?

Tortilla Man. Why do you ask so many questions? Just look around. Open your eyes and really see. We're flying over the Rio Grande now.

Carlos. We are??? (*He jumps around and makes the Flying Tortilla take a nose dive*).

Tortilla Man. I wouldn't do that if I were you, Carlossssss . . . (The Tortilla Man *looks nervous, but quickly regains control of the ship.* Carlos *holds on for dear life. He is glued to the firm spongy mass under him and stares, wide-eyed. The Flying Tortilla is a flat spongy disc about six feet across and four feet wide. It is a blue color, with multicolored spots. Tough and durable, it has been made by a Master Tortilla Maker,* Mr. Juan *himself. It has no seats to speak of, just two slightly raised air pockets that serve as seats.* The Tortilla Man *is wearing a historical costume of the fifteenth century, complete with armor. He looks proud and distinguished and a bit older than before. On the side of the Flying Tortilla is a flag of an unknown country with a feather on top. At the sides are rudders of dough. In the middle are several large sacks of baking powder, used to raise and lower the ship, much like the sand bags used in balloons. Once airborne, the Magic Blue Corn Tortilla floats on air currents and the occasional boost from various birds who happen to be flying by.*) You should never do that, Carlos!

Carlos. Are we on an airplane or a ship?

Tortilla Man. I must have asked questions, too, when I was a boy, so I'll have to be patient. Yes, we are on a ship. The Magic Flying Blue Corn Tortilla. There seems to be no satisfying you with answers . . . that's good. Yes, Carlos, right now we are . . . let me see . . (The Tortilla Man *looks at a compass, checks the feather, and moistens his finger with saliva, then holds it up a foot or so from his face.*) We are about two miles due west of Cuchillo as the birds fly.

Carlos (*embracing* The Tortilla Man *with a mixture of fear and glee*). We are?

Tortilla Man. Boy, once you get over your wonder, you can start dealing with life. Sit up there . . . you're slouched over like you're afraid.

Carlos (*peering over the edge of the Flying Tortilla*). I am!

Tortilla Man. You, my young explorer, afraid of this . . . (The Tortilla Man *begins to jump up and down on the tortilla*).

Carlos (*begging* The Tortilla Man *to stop*). Oh please, Mr. Juan, won't you stop doing that? I think I'll just sit here, if you don't mind.

Tortilla Man. This isn't like you, Carlos. We're on an adventure. You just can't sit there and watch the birds fly by. You have to jump in or, in this case, fly on . . .

Carlos. How far up are we?

Tortilla Man. About three cloud lengths and a half . . . I can check . . . (*He makes a motion to go to the back of the ship.*)

Carlos. No, that isn't necessary. Is this . . . a . . . tortilla?

Tortilla Man. Nothing but the best for me . . . blue corn.

Carlos. How does it fly?

Tortilla Man. Up, Carlos, up! Now then, here we have the front and lateral rudders. I had a lot of trouble perfecting them. It seems the birds would fly by and nibble on them between meals. Lost a lost of rudders that way. I used to carry a parachute for safety. But since I've put those letters on the side, it's been better.

Carlos. M.F.T.V.F. What does it mean, Mr. Juan?

Tortilla Man. Glad to see you relaxing, Carlos. I hate to see tense young people. Why, those letters mean MAGIC FLYING TORTILLA VERY FATTENING. Birds are very conscious of their figures. To an extreme you might say.

They never stop talking about it, but oh, how they love to eat! You don't do that, do you, Carlos?

Carlos. Do you really talk to the birds?

Tortilla Man. Yes, and usually in a loud voice. They're hard of hearing. I talk to them when I have time. We're always so busy. Now for the rest of the tour. How you do ask questions! The best thing is not to ask but to listen. You'll find out things much faster that way. Not enough listening these days. Here is my flag, Carlos. My compass and baking powder bags. (*He pauses and looks at* Carlos.) I'm waiting for questions.

Carlos. What flag is that?

Tortilla Man. Why it's my own, of course. It's the flag of growth. (*The flag is in burnt desert colors. It shows the mountains, the rivers, and the plants of the desert. In the forefront is a plant with its root system exposed.*) This is the land, dry and burnt. To someone who doesn't know its ways, it is like thirst—there is no in-between. Our land is a land of mountains and rivers, dry things and growing things. Our roots are in the earth and we feel the nourishment of the sky. This is *my* flag . . . what's yours?

Carlos. I don't have a flag of my own.

Tortilla Man. You don't? Well, then you shall have to make one.

Carlos (*discovering his box on the Flying Tortilla*). My cigar box! What is it doing here?

Tortilla Man. You were thinking about it, perhaps?

Carlos. Why, that's my feather up there with your flag!

Tortilla Man. I needed a compass. You see, birds tell the direction by the way their feathers blow, and besides, it's a nice feather.

Carlos. My father calls it an old ugly chicken feather.

Tortilla Man. Has he ever had his own feather? (Carlos *shakes his head no.*) Well, then, how would he know?

Carlos. It *is* an old feather!

Tortilla Man. Don't let the birds hear you say that. They may never forgive us! They don't exactly hold grudges, but it'll go better for us if we keep on their good side; the other side can be most uncomfortable. They give us a push now and then when the air current is low, so we can really use their help. You see, we fly by current. I ignite special minerals and then sprinkle that mixture over baking powder and whoosh! We are off! The staying up part is the only thing I've never really quite figured out yet.

Carlos. Ohhhh! (*He looks down fearfully.*) How do you land?

Tortilla Man. By dropping bags of powder much the way a balloon drops sand.

Carlos. But, Mr. Juan, that's not the way it works!

Tortilla Man. It isn't? Oh, what does it matter? Why must everything work the same way for everybody?

Carlos. All of this is hard to believe.

Tortilla Man. Just look down there . . . isn't it breathtaking? That's my trail down there. The Juan de Oñate Trail.[18] That's the way I came up through Mexico and all the way north to Santa Fe. When I came through here, there was nothing . . . Imagine that!

Carlos. Oñate, the explorer? We learned about him in school. He was from Spain, but he came up from Mexico to explore. He was a conquistador. I did a report on him.

Tortilla Man. Him? You mean me!

Carlos. You? But you're The Tortilla Man, Mr. Juan.

Tortilla Man. So I am.

Carlos. How can you be two people at once? Mexican and Spanish? Modern and old?

Tortilla Man. Carlos, my boy, when are you going to stop asking questions? Too many questions! (*He pushes out two bags of baking powder.*) We're going to land and walk around. (*He adjusts the compass.*) Now then, take a seat,

---

18. **Juan de Oñate Trail** (HUAN day ohn-YAH-tay) Oñate was a Spanish explorer who claimed New Mexico for Spain and was its first governor.

Carlos. The landing may be a bit rough. I think a bird heard you earlier.

Carlos. You mean about the feather?

Tortilla Man. Ssshhh! Birds are terrible spellers, so kindly spell out that word henceforth. Very good diction but lousy spellers. (*The Magic Tortilla floats down and lands on a rocky hill.*) I thought you'd like this place. I understand you collect fossils.

Carlos. Yes, I do!

Tortilla Man. Well, look around you, Carlos. We have some good ones here. This used to be under water many, many years ago. All of this was once part of a great vast ocean.

Carlos. Where are we now?

Tortilla Man. It's hard to believe, I know, but we are at the bottom of the sea! Find your fossil. We have all the time in the world. Find your fossil!

[*They stand together a moment.* Carlos *picks up a fossil and puts it in his cigar box. They wander about collecting fossils for a while and then reboard the ship and head due north to an area of white sand.* The Tortilla Man *has brought a lunch, and they take a break. They collect some sand, which* Carlos *puts in his box, then head back to Cuchillo.*]

Tortilla Man. It's getting late, Carlos. Are you tired? We must go on . . .

Carlos. I could never be tired with you, Mr. Juan. I'm too happy.

Tortilla Man. You're a good boy, Carlos.

Carlos. That's the problem! I don't want to be a good boy! I want to be a person. Nobody really likes good boys.

Tortilla Man. That *is* a problem. I see what you mean. It seems you can't be too good or too bad. It's hard. The solution is just to be yourself. Be truthful, and you won't have to worry about being at any far end. You'll be in the middle with yourself.

Carlos. But it's so hard!

Tortilla Man. When will you learn not to be impudent, boy! Trust me, and trust yourself above all. Here we are!

[*They drag the Flying Tortilla with a rope that is attached. They then sit by the side of the river, happy but exhausted.*]

Carlos. I want this time to last forever!

Tortilla Man. It will, my friend, but shhh! Let's listen to the birds. They're talking . . . see, there they are on the Magic Flying Tortilla. . . .

[*The* Four Old Women, *now* Birds, *peck at the Flying Tortilla.*]

Ton. I'm hungry, Tin . . .

Tin. Me too, Ton.

Tan. I haven't eaten in days.

Mabel. Weeks . . .

Ton. Months . . .

Tin. Years . . .

Tan. When was it, anyway?

Mabel. When The Flying Tortilla Man was on his way South . . .

Ton. I don't know if I would have lasted if he hadn't come by . . .

Tin. I was dying for even a moldy, dried-out crust, a few crumbs . . . anything!

Tan. How about a nice big juicy earthworm?

Mabel. I'm a vegetarian.

Ton. Against your religion, eh?

Mabel. No, against my waistline.

Tin. Always prancing about with her airs she is!

Ton. Look who's talking!

Tin. What about you, Ton-Tona?

Ton. Don't call me that, please.

Tin. Against your religion?

Tan. Oh, yes, a nice big juicy baked earthworm would be nice, with lots of gravy and a bird's nest salad . . . (*She cries out.*) Bird does not live by bread alone!

Mabel. Stop it! I feel faint!

Tan. Can it be? Can it be? Oh, dear, The Tortilla Man is coming back this way. He's spotted us. See him, Mabel? Girls, take courage. Here he comes. (*They all bow.*) Oh, great Tortilla Man!

Ton. Image of hope, blessed Tortilla!

Tin. Blessed be the Holy Name of Tortilla!

Mabel. Thank you, Mr. Juan. (*She stuffs her face with some tortilla.*) Food!

Tin. Now who's watching her figure?

Tan. Not me, I don't have problems!

Ton. Nor me!

Mabel. You're all as crazy as magpies!

Tin. That's a terrible insult, Mabel!

Tan. Will you be quiet! They're just about ready to take off, and I'm still hungry! I'm still so hungry I can't think or move!

Ton (*speaking to the others*). She never could!

Mabel. Girls, please, we have to be off. Mr. Juan is nearly ready to leave. Settle down and get in formation. That's right!

[*They dress right and do a drill. Then, they fly off.*]

Birds. Thank you, Mr. Juan!

Tortilla Man (*as he inspects the ship*). Rudders don't look too damaged. Really, those birds are all right, Carlos. They do give me a push now and then. Now hop aboard . . . we have to go home.

Carlos. Do we have to, Mr. Juan?

Tortilla Man. We have things to do. We have our work, our families. And there's the fiesta coming up. I have to get ready for that.

Carlos. I don't have a real family, and I'm so tired of making tortillas!

Tortilla Man. There you go again. It's not what you do but how you do it. And as for having a family, you have people who love you . . . and you have yourself. So many people don't have themselves, Carlos. So what does it matter how many brothers and sisters you have? Why all of us are brothers and sisters!

Carlos. I've heard all those things before!

Tortilla Man. Yes, but did you listen to them? Or ask yourself *why* people were saying such things? Now be still with yourself and don't talk about you know what—because our friends might be listening. They might think we're saying one thing when we really mean another. Carlos, are your tired? Rest there on the Magic Tortilla. Before you know it, we'll be in Cuchillo. Close your eyes, sleep, sleep!

[Carlos *is getting sleepy, almost against his will.*]

Carlos. I'm not really sleepy. It's been the happiest day of my life!

Tortilla Man. Stretch out there and rest!

Carlos. Just for a moment, Mr. Juan. A little nap, that's all I need. You won't leave me, will you?

Tortilla Man. No, I won't leave you, ever . . . remember these things, Carlitos, and sleep, sleep . . .

Carlos (*in a far away voice*). Mr. Juan, where's my box? I had it right here . . .

Tortilla Man. Sleep . . . you need it, boy, to be strong . . .

Scene 4

*O*utside *the factory the next morning.* Carlos *wakes to find himself in the same position he was in on the Flying Tortilla. His body is cold and cramped. He is surprised to find himself on the steps of the tortilla factory.* Tudi *shakes him as* Oscar *and* Elias *stand nearby.*

Tudi. Wake up! Wake up, you rascal!

Carlos. Mr. Juan, where is my box? I had it right here.

Elias. There you are, Tudi. He admits his guilt.

Oscar. It was Carlos who broke into your office, Tudi, and tried to get in the safe.

Elias. Oscar and I were walking by and noticed the lights were still on. Then we saw Carlos sleeping here. That's when we called you, Tudi.

Tudi. Thank you, boys! I'll make it up to you. Fortunately, the snake wasn't able to get into the safe, but he sure made a mess of things. How did you get in, Carlos? Oh, you're going to be sorry that you ever saw this place. You'll never forget this day!

Carlos. I don't understand. I was with Mr. Juan!

Elias. Don't lie to us, you thief!

Oscar. He's a sneaky one. Don't believe him, Tudi.

Elias. I'm very surprised, Tudi. He always seemed so good.

Carlos. I don't understand all this . . . what's happening?

Tudi. Don't lie to me, Carlos. And here I was thinking of promoting you. Vandal, you broke into my office and tried to rob my safe; and when you couldn't break in, you made a mess of things!

Elias. And you dropped this . . . (*He shows off* Carlos's *cigar box.*)

Carlos. My box, where did you find it?

Oscar. He admits it! Remember this, Elias. We're witnesses!

Elias. We'll sue! Won't we, Tudi?

Tudi. We'll sue! You'll be sorry you were ever born. They'll probably send you to the boys' home in Springer.

Oscar. Not that!

Elias. That's where all the hardened criminals go. A cousin of mine is there, so I know.

Carlos. You're all wrong! I wasn't here at all. I was flying with Mr. Juan.

Elias. Who is this Mr. Juan, anyway?

Carlos. He's a friend of mine.

Oscar. Listen to that story, would you, Tudi!

Tudi. Stop lying to us, Carlos. You're making up these crazy stories to lead us off the track.

Carlos. You've got it all wrong. I can show you. Give me the box, please.

Elias. Oh no, that's important evidence.

Oscar. If you were flying around, show us your wings. Show us your wings! That's a funny one!

Tudi. Let's go!

Carlos. Where? I'm not guilty. I tell you, I'm not guilty!

Tudi. This is a matter for the Sheriff's Office.

Oscar (*he turns to* Carlos, *almost impressed*). You little thief, you've hit the big time!

Elias. Is Fatty in today? I thought he went fishing on Wednesdays.

Tudi. The law is always at hand.

Oscar. What does that mean?

Tudi. Sounds good, doesn't it?

Carlos. But you have it all wrong!

Oscar. Man, if I were you, I'd start praying. No one can face Fatty Campbell and not feel helpless fear.

Tudi. Go on, march. March, there. Go on, march! Oscar, you run ahead and tell Bertina and Hermano Gil. They'll want to hear about this. Tell them to meet us at the Sheriff's Office. Forward now, to justice!

Scene 5

*T*he Sheriff's Office. It is near the Plaza on Calle del Sol [19] *street. It consists of several rooms. The lobby has a desk and chairs and a long, orange plastic couch for visitors. A magazine rack is near the couch and has old copies of* Ford Times, The Ranch News, *and last Thursday's paper. On the wall is a calendar from Corney Hawkins Olds. Next to that is a Navy picture of Company 1435, U.S. Naval Training Center, Great Lakes, Illinois, and beside that is a horseshoe and a picture of President John F. Kennedy.*

---

19. *Calle del Sol* (KEYE-ay del SOHL) Sun Street

Fatty. Where were you the night of the 10th?

Carlos. With Mr. Juan.

Elias. There he goes again with that fabulous story.

Fatty (*He admonishes* Elias). Whoa there, boy. Order in the court. What do you mean speaking out of turn!

Elias. Tell us the truth now, Carlos!

Carlos. I *have* been telling the truth.

Bertina. No child of mine was ever a disgrace to our home, son.

Hermano Gil. Please, Carlos, tell Mr. Fatty the truth.

Fatty. Order, order in the court! (Elias, Bertina, Hermano Gil *and the others settle down and look at* Fatty.) Ahem. It's about time. (*To* Carlos) Were you not found near the scene of the crime by these two young fellows? (*He peers at* Elias *and* Oscar *very closely.*) I think I know you two from somewhere.

Carlos. Yes, I was, Mr. Fatty. I fell asleep with Mr. Juan, and he must have carried me back to the factory.

Fatty. *Who* is this mysterious Mr. Juan?

Hermano Gil. Pay no attention to him, Sheriff.

Elias. He keeps talking about a Mr. Juan who flies.

Tudi. He's unstable. That's all there is to it. He needs help.

Bertina. Oh, shut your mouth, Tudi.

Hermano Gil. Bertina, my love . . . Bert, settle down.

Carlos. Mr. Juan is a friend of mine.

Tudi. It's all your fault, Bertina! I shouldn't have listened to you and given the boy a chance at the factory. Now look what he's done! He's ruined my business.

Bertina. It's not *your* business, you little toad. Nothing was stolen, your honor.

Hermano Gil. My love, please.

Fatty. Settle down, folks. I know emotions run high, but this is a court of law . . . and I am the law. Settle down there, folks!

Hermano Gil. Can we settle this out of court, Mr. Fatty?

Cotil. Of course not, Papa! This is a matter of public concern.

Hermano Gil. Nothing was stolen except a bag of frozen tamales . . . that's all . . .

[Elias *looks at* Oscar, *who shrugs his shoulders as if to say, "I was hungry."*]

Tudi. That's all! I'll sue, Gil. My reputation is ruined. Have you seen that mess in the office? I'll sue! I'll sue!

Fatty. Whoa there. As judge and jury, I take the reins of the law in my hands. Having viewed the evidence and spoken to the accused and the witnesses, I now proclaim the verdict of this court, Filmore P. Campbell presiding, this eleventh day of June, in the year of, etcetera. Isn't it about time for lunch, Gil? What time do you have?

Bertina. He's just a boy! He never meant to hurt anyone. He's a good boy, your honor.

Elias. So what's the verdict?

Fatty. Don't I know you from somewhere, sonny?

Cotil. Mama, we have to abide by the verdict.

Hermano Gil. I can't believe a boy of mine could do this. How could you, son?

Carlos. Papa . . . you must believe me . . . I'm innocent!

Elias. As innocent as a snake!

Cotil. He's a liar, Papa. Don't you know that already?

Elias. Sentence him!

Oscar. Show no mercy!

Fatty. I hereby sentence you, Carlos Campo, to a week's labor on the Plaza, early curfew, and a fine of twenty dollars for court costs. Case closed. We have the fiesta coming up, and we'll need all the help we can get. Report at five a.m. to Fernando at the water tower. Court dismissed. (*He speaks to* Elias.) I know you from somewhere. Don't you have a cousin . . . ?

Elias. You must be thinking of someone else, Mr. Fatty.

Tudi. I demand a retrial! Who's going to clean up my office? What about the tamales? My mother made them for me, and I was taking them home. I demand a retrial!

Fatty. Go back and sell a few tortillas!

Tudi. I'll sue!

Bertina. He's just a child! Can't you understand that?

Fatty. Clear the court . . . clear the court. It's my lunchtime. Someone mention tamales?

Tudi. *This* is justice?

Fatty. Insulting the court—five dollars!

Tudi. I'll write my congressman.

Fatty. Threatening the law—ten dollars.

Tudi. Now wait a minute!

Fatty. Harassing the court—fifteen dollars.

Elias. Man, Tudi, you better leave while you can. It doesn't look good for you.

Hermano Gil. After all these years, son, how could you break your father's heart? You were my only hope, Carlos. I felt as if you were my true son, my flesh and blood. Now you're a stranger!

[*He walks away with* Bertina *and* Cotil, *who is gloating.*]

Cotil. Papa, I told you he was a sneak!

Carlos. Papa! I'm innocent!

Hermano Gil. Don't talk to me. Let's go, Bert.

Bertina. That's all right, son. Dinner's at six. We're having papitas con chorizo.[20]

Hermano Gil. How can anyone eat with a mouthful of sand?

Cotil. Hey, Carlos, bad luck!

Elias. Where are you going now, Cotil?

Cotil. I'm busy. I'm going home with Mama. So don't you bother me.

Elias. How can you say that to me after all I've done for you?

Cotil. You were always too young for me.

Oscar. Hey Elias, I know something we can do.

Elias. Leave me alone, man.

Oscar. So what happened to our friendship?

---

20. **papitas con chorizo** (pah-PEE-tahs kohn choh-REE-soh) potatoes with sausage

Elias. I have better things to do. Out of my way.

[*They all exit.* Carlos *and* Fatty *are left in the courtroom.*]

Fatty. Come on, sonny, cheer up. It's not the end of the world. When I was a kid, I got into a few scrapes. What's it matter, huh? You want part of a tuna fish sandwich? Some chips? Now, cheer up. Here's the evidence. Don't tell anyone I gave it back to you. Run along now. I haven't got all day. I haven't eaten my lunch yet. Now, sonny, you watch those stories . . . they'll get you in a mess of trouble.

Carlos. They aren't stories . . . it's the truth! It's really the truth!

Scene 6

Carlos's *room late that night. He is sitting on the bed, when he decides to get up and get his box from the chest of drawers.*

Carlos (*looking up at the ceiling*). Where were you, Mr. Juan, when I needed you? Where are you now? Why do you always leave me? (*Dejectedly*) I am as lonely and sad as the day the men from the church carry the body of God around the Plaza in that wooden box on Good Friday. The people are all in black, singing with dried voices and moaning to themselves. They stop in front of doors that are closed. He said many things but not where he was from or where he went. He comes and goes, and I want to be angry with him, but I can't. I can feel him close sometimes, when it matters. He knows, he really knows me . . . and he cares. Mr. Tortilla Man, come back. Stay awhile with your Carlos. He needs friends. Because people hate him when he is good and love him when he is bad. (*He looks down at the cigar box.*) Should I open it? What of our fossils and sand? Will they be there? (*He opens the box.*) Where are they? What's this? It's a little note. "Remember, Carlos.

Your friend, Mr. Juan, The Flying Tortilla Man." That's all, just a note and this—a small hard edge of tortilla. Of what use is it? (*He throws the tortilla away and then retrieves it.*) Oh, well. It's something! He said many things, but not where he came from and where he went. He said many things . . . "Remember," he said, "remember." But what? What?

[Carlos *goes to sleep and has fitful dreams. The* Old Woman/Birds *call out his name in a dream sequence. "There he is . . . who . . . ," and he sees all the people from the court scene. He wakes up in a sweat, clutching the cigar box; then he drifts off to sleep again.*]

Scene 7

*T*he next morning in the Plaza. Carlos *is sweeping the bandstand. He looks forlorn and miserable.* Nora *comes up to him.*

Nora. What's wrong with boy?

Carlos. Hello, Nora.

Nora. What's wrong with Carlitos?

Carlos. I lost my job.

Nora. So sad. I miss Carlos at job. Oscar and Elias no like Nora—make fun all time. Neno? Neno?

Carlos. He's still very sick.

Nora. Neno! I look for him last night. Saw Oscar and Elias at the job.

Carlos. What was that, Nora?

Nora. Neno good boy—lose job? I look for him last night after Carlos walk Nora home. See Oscar and Elias make mess.

Carlos. They said I tried to break into Tudi's office last night.

Nora. Oh no, no. Oh no, that Elias and Oscar do.

Carlos. No, Nora. They said that about *me.*

Nora. Oscar and Elias go in and throw things around.

Carlos. What are you saying?

Nora. Nora see them.

Carlos. Have you told anyone?

Nora. I tell you. Nora see Elias and Oscar make mess.

Carlos (*grabbing her hand*). Let's go, Nora. Let's go see Fatty!

Nora. I don't know Fatty.

Scene 8

*T*he Sheriff's Office.

Fatty. This is a highly unusual case. I've taken the liberty to call in two witnesses.

Carlos. Nora told us how she saw Elias and Oscar break into Tudi's office and throw things around.

Fatty. That's fine, son; but what proof do we have?

Carlos. Nora told us! She's a witness!

Fatty (*taking* Carlos *aside*). Son, she's not well. Loca en la cabeza.[21] You know what I mean? I think she made it up to help you. (*He speaks to* Oscar *and* Elias.) What do you boys say?

Elias. Carlos is trying to defend himself. It was a good try, but it won't work.

Nora. Oscar with Elias.

Oscar. Go away, Nora.

Nora. She see. She see. Elias call Oscar stupid fat boy behind his back.

Elias. Don't listen to her, Oscar. She's not all there.

Nora. Elias hate Oscar. He told me. (*She looks at* Oscar.) Say that night that you a stupid boy and he smart one.

Elias. Don't believe her, Oscar!

Oscar. Well, how do you like that! After all we've been through! You never did like me, man. He was there, Fatty. He made me do it!

---

21. **Loca en la cabeza** (LOH-kah ayn lah kah-BAY-sah) crazy in the head

Elias. You stupid fool! Why'd you take those tamales? I told you not to!

Oscar. I was hungry! Fatty, it was Elias's idea. He told me about it and asked me to help. We were trying to get back at Carlos for being such a baby. I thought Elias was my friend, but he's the type that talks about you behind your back. He's just a lousy tortilla bum with the rot!

Elias. Will you shut up!! He's the sick one, Sheriff. He's got the rot. He's making things up!

Oscar. I'm smarter than you, Elias, you little punk. I can pick any lock I want to. What can you do besides give directions and tell people what to do? What do you know, anyway?

Nora. Carlos come back to work now?

Carlos. I was innocent all the time, Mr. Fatty.

Fatty. So it seems. The law is never tricked. Justice rules. Call Bertina, Gil, and Tudi. Court's in session. The retrial is about to begin.

Carlos. Why did you do this, Elias?

Elias. It was Cotil's idea. She made me do it. She wanted to get back at you for everything.

Oscar (*looking at* Carlos). You were always a better friend to me than Elias, Carlos.

Carlos. It's all right, Oscar. I forgive you.

Oscar. It was Elias's fault. He's full of poison blood.

Elias. It's the rot, man. I got the rot! It was Cotil made me do it . . .

Carlos. I forgive you too, Elias.

Elias. You always talked too much, Nora.

Nora. Thank you, all my friends! Go to work now?

Scene 9

*T*he *Fossil beds.* Carlos *and* The Tortilla Man *are sitting on a rock shelf reviewing the past few days' events. It is a peaceful twilight in New Mexico.*

Carlos. And so, Mr. Juan, everything finally worked out. Where were you all that time? You could have told the Sheriff that I wasn't guilty.

Tortilla Man. When will you learn not to be impudent, boy? The truth of the matter is that I was getting ready for the fiesta, and anyway, you handled things pretty nicely.

Carlos. I don't know what I would have done without Nora.

Tortilla Man. I told her to take care of you.

Carlos. Do you know her?

Tortilla Man. Oh, blessed tortillas, yes! We're dear old friends. And besides, I was with you all the time. Remember that night you looked inside your cigar box? You were thinking of me, and I heard you. I said hello. I'm sorry I had to take the sand and the fossil. You see, I thought it was the best way. Things can't be too easy for us, or we don't appreciate them. We don't grow that way! Here's your fossil and the sand. (The Tortilla Man *hands them to* Carlos.) Remember me when you see them.

Carlos. Will you go away before the fiesta, Mr. Juan? Neno was to play the part of the Indian scout, Jusephe,[22] but he's still a little weak, so they asked me to take the role. This is my first time in the fiesta play. When I grow up, I want to play the part of Oñate. But how can anyone play that part, if you're the real Oñate? Why don't *you* play the part?

Tortilla Man. We'll have to work out something by that time, Carlos.

Carlos. Elias and Oscar have to work in the Plaza now, in my place, but the Sheriff is letting them take part in the parade. All of us have roles in the pageant play![23] Will you

---

22. Jusephe (hoo-SAY-fay) *n.* a Native American who served as a scout for Juan de Oñate on one of his expeditions

23. pageant play (PAJ-uhnt PLAY) an exhibition or a drama that celebrates a historic event or tells the history of a community

be in the parade? You said something about getting ready for the fiesta.

Tortilla Man. Oh, I have a very small part. Nothing that anyone couldn't play if they really wanted to.

Carlos. Will I see you?

Tortilla Man. If you don't, I shall be very sorry. Now, remember to see, not to look. I might seem a bit different from myself, but it's me. You can never really change a person inside, no matter what you do.

Carlos. Mama is making the costumes. Cotil is playing the part of a Señorita, but she still won't talk to me.

Tortilla Man. She'll get over it.

Carlos. Even if you're not good, some people still don't like you.

Tortilla Man. Remember what I said, we're all from the same country. We have the sky which covers our heads and the earth which warms our feet. We don't have time to be anywhere in between where we can't feel that power. Some people call it love. I call it I.W.A.

Carlos. I.W.A.? What does that mean?

Tortilla Man. Inside We're Alike. Now I must leave you.

Carlos. Can we go for a ride on the Flying Tortilla some time?

Tortilla Man. Anytime you like, Carlos.

[*The Magic Tortilla takes off with a huge blast, and soon* Carlos *and* The Tortilla Man *are floating in space. Flash to the Plaza, the town fiesta, in honor of the founding of Cuchillo by Don Juan de Oñate. The Plaza is decorated with bright streamers and flowers, and booths completely circle it. There are food booths as well as game booths. The parade begins at North Cotton Street. First come the Spanish soldiers in costume, with* Tudi *leading.* Elias *and* Oscar *wear a cow costume and are led by a radiantly beautiful* Nora. Hermano Gil *plays the part of one of Oñate's generals, and* Bertina *is a noblewoman. She is followed by* Cotil, *and behind* Cotil *is* Fatty, *in a tight-fitting suit of armor and a helmet with the insignia of the Spanish army. He is the Master of*

Ceremonies. The parade marches forward. Jusephe, played by Carlos, *leads the Royal Entourage.*[24] Carlos *is followed by Don Juan de Oñate* (The Flying Tortilla Man), *a small old man with twinkling eyes.*]

Elias. Hey, Oscar, who's that old man next to Carlos?

Oscar. Let me see. (Oscar *sticks his head out of the cow's rear end.*) That's El Boss, Señor López—he owns the factory. He lives at one of those rest homes, but every year he comes out and plays Oñate. He's been doing it as long as I can remember.

Elias. So that's the original Tortilla Man, eh? He looks as old as the hills and as dusty.

Oscar. I can't go on much longer . . . it's hot!

Elias. So go work in an ice plant. Get it? Man, you have no sense of humor.

Oscar. You wouldn't have a sense of humor if you were back here!

[*They march forward, and when* Fatty *gets to the bandstand, he makes an announcement.* Carlos *sees* Neno *and yells to him.* Neno *is sitting on the side, resting in the sun, and looks much better.*]

Carlos. Hey, Neno! Neno, how are you?

Neno. I'm getting better, Carlos . . . I'm going to make it!

Elias. Move over, Oscar. There's Neno. I don't want germs to float over this way.

Nora. Come on, little cow; go see Neno.

Oscar. Can't you do anything, Elias? She's going near you-know-who-with-you-know-what. The Rot!

Nora. Neno, Neno!

Fatty. As Master of Ceremonies and Sheriff of the Cuchillo Municipality, I, Filmore P. Campbell, welcome you inhabitants to our annual fiesta in honor of the founding of Cuchillo by Don Juan de Oñate.

---

24. *Royal Entourage* (ROI-uhl ahn-too-RAHZH) a group of attendants to a king, queen, or other leader

[*The crowd cheers, and there is a great noise of firecrackers and shouts.* The Birds *are seen from a distance, viewing all the festivities.*]

Mabel. There he is . . .

Tin. Who?

Tan. The boy.

Ton. Are you going to start that again?

Mabel. I don't know what you're talking about.

Tan. What are they doing down there?

Tin. Who?

Mabel. The people in the Plaza.

Tan. They're laughing and having a good time.

Tin. You mean the ones out there? (*She peers into the audience.*)

Mabel (*looking out as well*). Oh, yes, they've been here awhile, haven't they?

Tan. I think they've had a good time, too. Don't you, Ton?

Ton. They look a little happier than when they came in.

Tin. Do you think so?

Tan. But what about the people in the Plaza? What's all that about down there? That parade and all the noise?

Mabel. Horses make me nervous.

Ton. Everything makes you nervous or unhappy or fat.

Mabel. I like a good story now and then, something to pass the time.

Ton. Oh, you and your time!

Tan. It's so nice to just sit here and smell the sky and the sunshine, and feel the sounds of life . . .

Mabel. How can you smell the sky, you crazy bird? You have it all mixed up!

Ton. Leave Tan alone, Mabel. She's all right. She's just being Tan.

Mabel. I guess you're right. She just can't help being Tan. Poor dear!

Tin. Are they getting nervous out there? (*Referring to the audience*)

Ton. No, but I think it's time to go home now.

Tin. Why? I was having so much fun!

Ton. It's just time.

Tan. Will we come back here again?

Tin. We'd better. I'm getting hungry just thinking about it.

Mabel. What are you silly birds talking about?

Tan. What's all the noise about anyway?

[*They fly off.*]

Ton. When will you listen, silly bird?

Tan. What was that? I couldn't hear you! "Listen." Did you say, "listen"? (*In a faraway voice*) Can't you just smell the sky?

AFTER YOU READ

Exchanging Backgrounds and Cultures

1. Why do you think Chávez includes the Chinese proverb at the beginning of the play? How does this relate to the play's opening scene? How does it relate to the fiesta and parade in the last scene?

2. What does the Tortilla Man symbolize? What does his flag suggest about his view of life?

3. Which of the many things the Tortilla Man tells Carlos are most important to you? Why?

What Do You Think?

Which character, event, or scene in the play appeals most to you? Why is this aspect of the play so meaningful to you?

Experiencing Drama

In this play, Chávez mixes fantasy with reality to present her views about life. She uses a setting that is familiar to her and allows one of the characters to learn from another character. Think about something new you have learned. Did someone else teach you about this? Write a short scene to show that lesson through the characters you create. You might try to use a magical character. Be sure to include stage directions and dialogue.

Optional Activity The parade at the end of the play reflects Mexican and Spanish history and culture. Think about a parade you have marched in or seen in which the culture of people plays an important role. Write a short scene that describes the parade. Provide details about the setting and costumes, and include dialogue for your characters.

UNIT 4: FOCUS ON WRITING

Although dramas are enjoyable to read, they are written to be seen and heard—to be performed. Some plays have only one setting and few characters. Other plays, like *The Flying Tortilla Man*, have different settings and many characters. When Chávez directed a production of this play in 1975, she used movable boards painted with scenery to create the settings.

Writing a Dramatic Scene

A scene has the same form as a full-length play, with a beginning, a middle, and an end. Write a dramatic scene about a family gathering, a historical event, or another topic of your choice.

The Writing Process

Good writing requires both time and effort. An effective writer completes a number of stages that together make up the writing process. The stages of the writing process are given below to help guide you through your assignment.

Prewriting

Brainstorm for ideas you might want to write about, and organize them in a list. After you choose your topic, consider what your message is and what you want your readers to learn from it.

Before you write, think about the setting and characters. Make notes about the time of year and place. Prepare a list of characters and write a brief description of each one. If you look at *The Flying Tortilla Man*, you will notice that the characters' ages are listed. Chávez includes character descriptions in the opening stage directions for Scene 1.

When choosing the setting and events, remember that you must be able to present them on stage. Try to avoid situations that may be too difficult to reproduce. List the props, or movable objects, and costumes you might need.

At this point, you can make an outline of the plot. Where does the scene begin? Who is the main character? What problem does he or she face? How is this character's conflict resolved? How does the scene end?

Drafting and Revising

Refer to your lists and plot outline as you write the first draft of your scene. Remember that your first draft will not be perfect. You can revise it in later drafts.

After your list of characters, write stage directions that will allow a reader to imagine the setting easily and a director and actors to know exactly how you want your scene to look.

Use the play format to begin writing the dialogue. Place a character's name at the left of your page, followed by a colon, and then write the character's words. You can include additional stage directions about action or tone of voice in parentheses within parts of the dialogue.

Once you finish your first draft, read it aloud so you can hear how the words will sound on a stage. Does the dialogue sound like natural conversation? Get a clear picture of the characters in your mind. Would they say the things you have written? Revise any parts you feel do not sound natural or do not convey what you intended. Eliminate anything that is unrelated to the scene.

Proofreading and Publishing

The proofreading stage involves correcting errors in spelling, grammar, punctuation, and capitalization. Review your scene and make any necessary corrections. Then, prepare a neat final copy.

Now your work is ready for the stage! Choose actors from among your classmates and perform the scene for other classes in your school.

LITERATURE ACKNOWLEDGMENTS

ART ACKNOWLEDGMENTS

cover: **Estudiantes Leiendo** (Students Reading), Tony Ortega, mixed media, 1992.

p. 3: **Tamalada**, Carmen Lomas Garza, copyright 1987 Carmen Lomas Garza. Photographed by Wolfgang Dietze.

p. 39: **Sueño de Sonia** (Sonia's Dream), Sam Coronado, © Sam Coronado, artist.

p. 81: **Cuatro Parejas Folkloricas** (Four Couples Folk Dancing), Tony Ortega, © Tony Ortega, artist.

p. 99: Fresco, Diego Rivera (Mexican 1886-1957), *Stern Hall, University of California, Berkeley.* Painted at Sigmund Stern home, Atherton, California, April 1939. Photograph by Don Beatty © 1983.